The
Worship

The Dark Worship

Toyne Newton

vega

Acknowledgments

Special thanks to: Debbie Benstead, Andy Collins, John Launden, Gerry and the healing group, Meriel and Ray for all their help and support; Geoff Meddle for late-night logging on; David Icke for having the temerity to publish works that would otherwise remain unseen; Lyn Morrison and John Tobler for their continued friendship and interest; and finally Stuart Booth for making it all happen... again.

Research: West Kennett Long Barrow and some additional material, courtesy of Charles Walker.

ISBN 1-84333-586-7

A catalogue record for this book is available
from the British Library

First published in 2002 by
Vega
64 Brewery Road
London, N7 9NT

A member of **Chrysalis** Books plc

Visit our website at www.chrysalisbooks.co.uk
Printed in Great Britain
by Creative Print and Design Wales, Ebbw Vale

Contents

Introduction

Criminologists are people who study crime, usually without ever participating in it themselves. In the area of occult studies, the same is true of my own investigations into the dark worship.

As a religious neutral who does not belong to any such related group or organization, I am probably in a more suitable position to assess the occult objectively. The word 'occult' means hidden. It has a dual nature, embodying both positive and negative aspects. Not everyone who practises rituals under its concealing cloak is involved with mystical organizations, and these groups are not necessarily malevolent in themselves.

However, the secret organizations scrutinized in this book do play a prominent part in the occult conspiracy. In addition, they should not be seen solely as practitioners of witchcraft, black magic or, indeed, satanism, but also as self-appointed occult overlords, who—together with their subordinates—possess an understanding of certain magical processes which they have apparently been attempting to appropriate in order to fulfil their own alleged aims of spiritual control over today's global societies.

Conventional historians, along with some other like-minded people, may well find that these extraordinary and sometimes disturbing disclosures are at variance with their own established viewpoints. This I acknowledge; all I ask is that they try and keep an open mind and assimilate this book's contents before coming to any conclusions. Furthermore, for those who are willing to rise above any belief system based on opinionated dogma, the information contained in this book will, I hope, provide a new awareness which in itself will be a powerful weapon for combating the dark worship.

TOYNE NEWTON

Chapter 1
The Gathering Chaos

What we might call the 'matrix of magic' is a globalized, if loosely interlinked, network of groups and individuals, many of them using the Internet as an information and communication centre.

Among these people are those who seek to debase the 'Ancient Wisdom', rooted in pre-Christian, pagan times, and turn it into what is referred to gloomily as the 'Dark Worship'. Some openly have websites on the Internet; others remain shadowy and secretive as they practise their malign craft. Such groups are, apparently, operating in Great Britain, continental Europe, South Africa and the USA.

My investigations into such portentous matters began a generation ago, with a baffling local mystery.

The Manifestation
In the autumn of 1975, the *Littlehampton Gazette*, published in Sussex, England, printed a news story that disclosed the latest extraordinary occurrence in a quite astonishing sequence of paranormal incidents. These had gripped the south of England, gaining coverage on the BBC's *Nationwide* programme and national radio.

Prompted by the inexplicable disappearance of two dogs in Clapham Woods, West Sussex, earlier in that same year, as well as by an inordinate number of reported UFO sightings in the area, members of a UFO investigation group decided to take a thorough look at events.

They visited the weird woodland, equipped with a Geiger counter, compass and other items essential to their profession, and, as they retraced their steps along a footpath they came across a mysterious footprint which they had not seen when they had earlier passed that way.

Four claw marks were clearly visible on one side of the print with another claw mark separately positioned to the rear. The footprint measured 8¼ inches

in length and 3⅞ inches in width. A similar print could be seen about 12 inches away from the first.

The group members took readings: the Geiger counter needle shot across to beyond danger level when held over the footprints, while the compass pointer reacted in a similar manner, spinning chaotically before regulating like a pendulum in a metronomic motion. Barely had the group had time to absorb this latest phenomenon when a vertical column of grey mist appeared before them and began to form into a huge bear-like shape, towering above the foliage in the woods. All this was taking place some 200 yards from the main A27 road's Titnore Lane junction (as it was then—the road has since been re-routed as part of a major redevelopment programme).

The manifestation remained visible for ten seconds before disseminating eerily along the footpath and fading away completely.

Since the 1960s—long before this incident—many people have reported accounts of paranormal incidents at this site; mostly they were people with no real interest in the subject matter, but who had nevertheless experienced perhaps their first—and usually only—encounter with the unknown. Experiences ranged from sudden bursts of powerful air currents to the spontaneous onset of stomach cramps, dizziness and even being pushed over by unseen forces. People talked of the woods as being a 'birdless grove': the lack of wildlife was noticeable.

Localized flashes of lightning or violent sparks were also seen at various times by local residents, and pet dogs were also affected, their owners reporting fits and other symptoms of acute fear and distress. Sudden drops in temperature in so-called 'cold spots' were accompanied by grey, misty forms; yet more paranormal experiences were reported by many different people during the mid to late 1970s.

Day of the Demon

Early in 1978, amid continued press speculation that 'something' was in the woods, the television station ITV sent a team to interview Charles Walker, who was conducting his own investigation into these mystifying matters quite independently of the ufologists.

Charles, whom I did not know at the time, had a strong hunch that an occult group was using the area, and later that year he began making discreet enquiries while publicly maintaining the UFO and paranormal lines of enquiry.

This stealthy approach paid off. One evening in November 1978 Charles received an intriguing telephone call from a well-spoken man, asking him to come immediately to a part of Clapham Woods known as the Crossroads, where four pathways intersect. At this potentially dangerous rendezvous in the pitch-black woods, a voice that Charles instantly recognized as that of the telephone caller spoke from the cover of thick foliage.

Warning Charles not to look for him in the interests of their mutual safety, the man claimed to be an initiate of the Friends of Hekate, a group formed in Sussex, England. He stated that the Friends of Hekate held monthly meetings in Clapham Woods. He alleged that obscene, diabolical magical rites regularly occurred at these meetings. He intimated that Charles was standing very close to a site that had been in use. Powerful people were apparently involved who would brook no interference. He declared that the Friends of Hekate had used the woods for the past ten years and would continue to use them for another ten before selecting another area in which to 'spread the word'. He ended by saying that the group would 'stop at nothing to ensure the safety of their cult'.

Any doubts Charles may have had concerning the authenticity of this daunting clandestine encounter were soon dispelled when he became the victim of a deliberate 'hit and run' incident some two weeks later while cycling home from work. He suffered head and back injuries, which affected him for several weeks afterwards. Here was evidence that the group would indeed countenance no interference in their affairs. Charles continued to probe gently, however, and the real breakthrough came when, acting on a hunch, he entered an unoccupied building in part of the Clapham Manor House complex, and discovered a huge demonic mural covering one of the walls.

Painted in brilliant colours, it was not an image that anyone could have copied from a book, because nothing like it exists in encyclopedias of demonology. It was not what might have been regarded as a usual or traditional devil image, and was, one had to assume, something special to the Friends of Hekate, possibly used as a backdrop for rituals. The mural was a crude but detailed piece of work. It depicted a large bald head, which had a feminine face with long ears and blue curled horns. Clearly seen on the face were red and black marks, representing the smearing of blood. In claw-like hands with razor sharp talons, the creature appeared to be holding a religious orb with an eight-armed cross and circle. The body was covered in reptilian scales and ended in a devilish forked arrowhead tail curving up over the back, and the whole was depicted against a vivid background of fire and flames. This demonic interpretation rendered other devil images sober by comparison.

Drawings, paintings and symbols—especially detailed ones—are an important part of the proceedings of a serious high magical order, and it was fast becoming apparent that the Friends of Hekate were indeed serious, with a malicious penchant for luring inquisitive investigators and then punishing them for getting too close.

Having photographed the mural, Charles promptly left—in the nick of time, as it happened, for a man suddenly appeared, shouting angrily, and gave chase; as he was carrying a shotgun Charles didn't stop to argue but made off homewards, knowing that he now had proof of the secret cult's existence—in the form of a photograph that some occult experts have deemed amongst the most important finds in British occult history.

Time Stood Still

It was during this period (1978–81) that John Launden, a down-to-earth builder, was undertaking restoration work on both Clapham and Patching churches for a well-established local firm, Chichester Steeplejacks. He began to find the atmosphere in and around the churches extremely strange—as indeed did all his workmates. Each day they all left for home before darkness fell, something they wouldn't normally do. Every time they drove into the carpark by Clapham Church and woods, it felt as though time itself had stood still. For the most part the villagers kept themselves to themselves, yet the steeplejacks had the constant feeling of being watched. The atmosphere was entirely disharmonious, and they found it quite unnerving.

The restoration work was finally completed in 1981. Mr Launden had worked on many churches throughout Sussex but had never before experienced a place like Clapham. A local psychic supported this view: he had visited the Clapham area several times but on each occasion, as he had approached the village from the main road, he had felt that he was entering a time vortex. The houses, gardens, rooftops and surrounding area appeared locked into the 13th century, even though the modern world was but a few hundred yards away.

The Power Spiral

In response to three articles I had written in *The Unexplained* magazine about the mysterious events at Clapham and subsequent similar paranormal phenomena at Chanctonbury Ring, I was contacted by Alan Brown, a Southampton-based writer who had information on these and other matters. Our meeting led us to decide upon a joint investigation with Charles Walker.

Our findings were eventually published in *The Demonic Connection* (Blandford Press, 1987). In this book we were able to provide, as far as we could, the first account of the secret activities of the Friends of Hekate, together with the Dark Goddess of the underworld from which the group had taken their name. We were also able to chronicle the wider implications of the demonic connection, concluding that the Friends of Hekate were working ancient sites and areas of prodigious magical potency for their own obviously malign purposes.

Ley power is probably best described as being akin to a psychic power grid, encompassing a mesh of subterranean forces and linear, overground energy paths that link with cosmic and atmospheric influences.

Man interferes with these powers, though, by building roads through the natural landscape or sinking mine shafts, and leys become cut or blocked; when this happens they are classified as 'black streams'.

Most occultists will acknowledge that there is only one force, which in essence is neutral. The nature of the force, however, is governed by the objectives of the magical operators who are attempting to utilize its considerable power.

Practitioners of wicca—witchcraft—will usually banish, after usage, any elemental that has been invoked. Only a corrupt order such as the Friends of Hekate would deliberately leave such thought forms on site as a psychic seal on their own hallowed ground. Any sensitive person stumbling across such elementals could be adversely affected, albeit only temporarily.

With all the paranormal phenomena being experienced by various people in Clapham Woods and nearby Chanctonbury Ring, it had become clear that the Friends of Hekate were no ordinary group. Our hypothesis, which had laid the blame firmly upon them, was borne out by an anonymous letter which had arrived in a batch together with several others in response to my article on the Clapham Woods mysteries (published in *The Unexplained* magazine before I had begun to write *The Demonic Connection*).

This letter claimed, among other things, that the Friends of Hekate group which used the Clapham Woods site was but one single cell operating within a network, which included other centres at Winchester, Avebury and London. A sinister central triad, which comprised two women and one man, apparently ran the group from London. The women were aged about thirty and sixty, and the man was about forty-five (this was in 1982).

They used a system of circles, or grades, which consisted of an inner circle of people and descended towards outer grades. This was a method of organization that had been used by powerful high magical orders down the centuries and was known as the 'malefic power spiral'.

It was a scheme that ensured the total security of the group by not revealing to neophytes on the outer grades what the precise nature of the group was, or even that there were other grades to ascend to, until they were judged to be entirely ready for proper initiation and could be fully trusted.

At the end of 1987 I was contacted by author and psychic researcher Andrew Collins, who, after reading *The Demonic Connection*, felt there was a strong link with the Friends of Hekate and his own investigation into the 'Black Alchemist' affair.

As severe gale-force winds lashed against the walls of my coastal home on January 2, 1988, I listened to Andrew recounting the extraordinary saga of the 'Black Alchemist'. Together with a powerful psychic named Bernard, Andrew had discovered that a corrupt adept using his own hybrid-bastardized form of alchemy, combined with ritual black magic, had been desecrating ancient sites and churches in Essex, Kent and East Sussex. These rituals involved the use of various artefacts inscribed with magical symbols and placed in the ground, thus creating a fortification of negative energies.

The Gestating Entity

It had taken the unique knowledge of Greco-Egyptian expert Terry du Quesne to decipher some of the symbols inscribed by the Black Alchemist on his stone artefacts, which confirmed that the rituals the adept was using to invoke arcane magical forces were actually over 1700 years old.

Among other symbols identified by Andrew Collins was the Monas hieroglyphic symbol, created and published in a book by the Elizabethan occultist Dr John Dee in 1564 and which was said to contain the ultimate formula for cabbalistic power. But through these rituals and the subsequent discovery of the objects, Bernard had become psychically linked to the debased adept and those who were working with him.

In October 1986, Bernard had 'become aware' of Clapham Woods in Sussex as a place that had been ritually used by a group who were working with the Black Alchemist. *The Demonic Connection* had, of course, not then been published, and Bernard possessed no prior knowledge whatsoever of the recent history of Clapham Woods and all the paranormal activities that were connected with it—yet he had psychically pinpointed the precise location of the Friends of Hekate as well as identifying their activities.

A game of cat and mouse was developing. The climax came with an incident at Danbury churchyard, Essex: on a bleak November night in 1987, Andrew Collins and Bernard discovered a black dagger speared through an animal heart and planted among the upturned roots of a hurricane-damaged horse-chestnut tree.

I studied the finely carved tribal dagger. Running my finger along the freshly cleansed blade to the point where it had pierced the bloody heart, I could clearly make out the arcane magical symbols inscribed on it by the perpetrators of this macabre ritual. The shiny black finish and the carved handle, in the shape of a crouching monkey, made it ideal for use as an 'athame' (a black-hilted knife) during magical ceremonies. The crouching monkey probably represented the *cynocephalus*, or yellow baboon, a hallowed breed that, in Ancient Egypt, betokened the dark or waning phase of the lunar cycle usually identified with the Dark Goddess, Hekate.

Bernard was sure that this act of iniquity was the work of the Hekate Order's high priestess, as she had linked up with the Black Alchemist for this ritual. The whole affair had had an adverse effect on Bernard: he had felt sapped of his natural energy, found himself staggering as if drunk, as if the very life force were being drained from him. Andrew had been inclined to think that the dagger's planting had been a deliberate act in order to ensnare Bernard in view of his having become psychically linked to these corrupt and dangerous magical operators. A closer look at the magical inscription etched into the dagger's blade revealed, however, an even more sinister motive— namely to induce symbolically the birth of a questionable entity or Antichrist, which would form inside the conceptual womb of Hekate.

That the Hekate group should be harbouring such notions suggested strongly that they were preparing some sort of negative agenda, some era of chaos and devastation.

Chaos and devastation of a physical kind had befallen Clapham Woods after the hurricane of October 16, 1987. The crossroads, and the Hekate site nearby, had been obliterated and the woodland decimated. North of Clapham a large round pit, sinister and situated above the mass graves of plague victims, had been filled in with the remnants of hurricane-damaged trees.

On a visit to Clapham in the late summer of 1989 I tried—with difficulty—to find the pit, and on eventually locating its whereabouts I discovered that it had been further covered by a fresh growth of foliage, enabling it to blend in with the rest of the surrounding woodland as if it hadn't existed at all; only a slight indentation in the surrounding soil marked the spot where the mysterious pit had once been. The Rites of Hekate call for a sacrifice to be made in a round pit—preferably situated over old graves.

As I scrutinized the remaining wooded area I could see that many of the old sites, pathways and places were gone. It was as if the Friends of Hekate had procured and delivered their own epitaph by invoking the hand of Hekate herself to reach down and raze their places of worship, thereby concealing— perhaps for all time—their once hallowed ground. On seeing the devastation for the first time, Andrew Collins and Charles had expressed similar sentiments. Now I had seen it for myself.

In 1978 an Initiate of the Friends of Hekate warned Charles Walker that after a ten-year period they would select another area in which to 'spread the word'.

Ten years later there seemed to be mounting evidence that the group had stuck to their intentions in this respect. The stage had been set for their next phase of malignant growth. But what form would that take? Where would it lead them, and what effect would it have on those who tried to track them?

As I was to discover, the answers lay not in attempting to find out where they were going but where they had come from.

This book is about the history and prehistory of the Dark Worship—its influence on and within society, its relevance to current events as we head out from the turn of the millennium, a period in time that many believe will be one of the most crucial in our history.

Chapter 2
Goddess of the Shadows

In *The Demonic Connection* (*op. cit.*) my researchers and I had provided a historical account, as far as we could, of Hekate, the Dark Goddess of the underworld. Since then more information has come to light concerning this little known but nonetheless significant deity.

The earliest account of Hekate that I could find was the conception of the Dark Goddess. In *The Astrology of Fate* Liz Greene recounts 'the creation of the world' and the birth of the 'great triple goddess'. In her archetypal form she was known as Eurynome, and her symbol was the Moon. But as the universal goddess she was alone, and after rubbing her hands together a serpent had emerged, with whom she had consented to love. This act had caused the birth of beasts and 'all manner of creeping things' to populate the earth. Eurynome was promptly overcome with shame at her over-indulgence and consequently killed the serpent, renaming it 'Death' and sending it underground.

But as a deed of equity, Eurynome exiled a 'mulberry-faced shadow of herself' to an underground existence together with the ghost of Death. Her dark shadow she called 'Hekate'. In her earthly form Eurynome became Rhea, who was associated with Crete and the cult of Zeus (her son).

In Greek mythology Hekate was honoured by Zeus, who gave her a portion of the underworld, the earth and the air. The sacrifices made to her were usually dogs—her favourite animals, for she was known as 'she who makes dogs shiver'; according to Robert Graves, author of *The Greek Myths*, she is linked to the Dog Star, Sirius. He writes: 'Hesiod's account of Hekate shows her to have been the original Triple Goddess, supreme in heaven, on earth and Tartarus, but the Hellenes emphasized her destructive powers at the expense of her creative ones—the lion, dog and horse were her heads ... the dog being the Dog Star, Sirius'.

Hekate's connection with the underworld was also recorded by the

Roman orator, writer and statesman Cicero, who maintained that the souls of the dead could be called forth at Lake Avernus in Campania, a grim and deserted spot sacred to Hekate. It was situated in the neighbourhood of Pozzuoli and surrounded by hills covered by woods and pitted with cavities. In fact the cave of the Cumaean sibyl can still be seen there today.

The Roots of Hekate

Hekate's cult is believed to have originated in Caria, a Persian province in West Asia Minor. The city of Idrias was originally called Hekatesia. In parts of Caria the worship of Hekate is said to be deep-rooted, with references to the annual festival 'of the key' which aspires to the mysteries of the lower world. The town of Lagina in what is now Turkey became her most favoured cult centre.

The ancient name of Hekate is derived from the Greek, meaning 'far off' or 'far-darting', given to her because of her mysterious and awesome attributes; it also comes from the figure '100' in Greek. A 'great year' of twice fifty months consists of two reigns, thus making 100 months. The Dogon tribe of West Africa often described the fifty-year orbital period of Sirius by counting it 'double'; the Ancient Greeks applied the same philosophy to their sacred durations—Hekate ('100') unites two denominations of fifty.

Hekate was also supposed to be able to compel the ghosts of dead, unburied souls to wander for 100 years. Some of the earliest accounts of Hekate in Greek literature describe the goddess as Titan-born and belonging to the older world.

Greek communities became hotbeds of Hekate worship. The land of Thessaly (north-eastern Greece) had developed an evil reputation for sorcery, apparently resulting from Hekate worship; its taint permeated deep into the soil, according to an account in 'Hekate's Cult' by L. R. Farnell (in *The Goddess Hekate* (1992), edited by Stephen Ronan).

The rites of Hekate involved the use of symbolical keys, portions of the human body—mainly old bones—and fire lamps. The Ancient Greek sorcerers also incorporated an instrument known as the 'rhombos', or witches' wheel, according to the Egyptian magician and author Rollo Ahmed. In his classic book *The Black Art* (1936), he tells us, 'As the wheel spun round, it was thought that influence was gained over certain people or circumstances'. A rhombus is, of course, better known in mathematical terms as an equilateral parallelogram. Hekate's far-off aspect is illustrated by accounts in *The Black Art*, which tells of 'Greek sorcerers casting spells from a distance chiefly by means of wax figures which were often made hollow so that written incantations could be placed within them'.

The Ancient Greeks possessed a magical alphabet containing a great number of invocations scribed in sacred ink. They believed that these invocations gained in strength the more they were repeated. The Greeks also aspired to numbers and their relation to magical rites involving feast days and dedications to the demons and gods. The odd numbers were applied more than the even ones in this respect.

Another wheel appliance that had been used for interpreting communiqués said to have come directly from Hekate was found at Pergamum in Asia Minor. It took the form of a three-legged bronze table, dated *c*. third Century AD, which was etched with depictions of Hekate. It contained a round plate divided into various segments, each one embracing magical symbols, and in addition to the plate, two rings. The apparatus was said to have been spun like a roulette wheel or wheel of fortune. The rotating rings would come to a standstill over certain symbols, denoting a message from the Dark Goddess.

In early literature, though, Hekate has remained very much a deity of mystery. Her roots and true disposition have remained veiled throughout the ages. In his book *The Geography of Witchcraft* (1958) the Christian occult historian Montague Summers explains, 'There is no mention of her in the Homeric epics, she has no legend, she has no genealogy, facts which are surely not without deep meaning when we consider the mysterious and secret cult of this awful power.'

The earliest references to Hekate in Greek literature are ascribed to Hesiod, who links her with Artemis and Iphigenia—the daughter of Agamemnon who was made a priestess of Artemis's cult. The Hekate tradition was particularly profound in Thrace (northern Turkey), and on the island of Samothrace (now called Samothraki) her cult was integrated with the occult rituals of the Cabiri, whose own worship is as mysterious and potent as that of Hekate.

In *Philoseudes*, by the second-century Greek satirist Lucian, a manifestation of Hekate, after she has been evoked, is described as 'terrible to see in the form of a woman, half a furlong high, snake-footed, snakes in her hair, a torch in her left hand, a mighty sword in her right.' As we have discussed, the hound was sacred to Hekate, and it was often said that black dogs appeared immediately prior to the coming of the Dark Goddess.

Montague Summers describes the cult of Hekate much as one might expect: 'Her rites were monstrous, but to be respected and revered; her worshippers were accursed but to be dreaded and placated; her prayers blasphemy; her sacrifices impious and terrible. It was in truth the very cult of hell.'

Arnobius states that Hekate was the mother of Saturn. She would invoke demons from the underworld, who resided in tombs near the blood of murdered persons, or indeed at crossroads—one of her favourite haunts: her triple aspect is said to derive from her role as Goddess of the Crossroads, which in Ancient Greece was a meeting of three ways.

The Dark-veiled Virgin

In his book *The Cult of the Black Virgin*, Ean Begg links the Black Virgin cult to Hekate, particularly in her role as 'the invincible Queen of the Dead'. February, the month of the dead, commences with Candlemas Eve on the first day of the month, followed by Candlemas itself on the second. This is known as the Feast of the Purification of the Blessed Virgin Mary, and is the oldest feast dedicated to the Virgin. Begg notes that as Hekate presides over purification rites, this is therefore an important time for her, too. In 472 this feast turned into a torchlight procession to honour Persephone (often identified with Hekate), and a goat and a dog were both sacrificed to the Wolf God.

The Black Virgin cult is said to represent an esoteric concept of the Virgin Mary. It was particularly apparent in France where statues of Black Virgins or Madonnas can be found in many churches or priories; these had, in many cases, previously been places of Cathar worship, or indeed ancient pagan shrines.

Black Virgins are believed to show the Virgin Mary as an incarnation of the Dark Goddess—her worship deriving from the gnostic adulation of the Mother Goddess and pagan mysteries.

However, there is another side to the Black Virgin cult, which also links it to underworld goddesses Hekate and Persephone. In *The Cult of the Black Virgin* Ean Begg also refers to a 'hidden initiatory aspect'; in the introduction he states, 'The story of the Black Virgin may also include a heretical secret with the power to shock and astonish even current post-Christian attitudes, a secret, moreover, closely involving political forces still influential in modern Europe'.

The Chaldean Connection

The Chaldean Oracles, which first appeared in the second century AD, were an anthology of pagan ritual oracles containing some nebulous and powerful dark imagery and disclosing information on ritual methods and procedure. There are those who perceive these teachings to have been a scripture of the highest order, though they were probably nearer to Gnosticism than anything else. It is believed that these oracles were created by a group of elders, one of whom used his son as a medium to respond to ritual questions while in a trance state, providing a direct channel to the gods themselves. The Chaldean hierarchical system is based on a complex structure involving seven worlds, seven planetary zones—including the sphere of fixed stars, which were believed by this ancient race to surround the earth.

However, Proclus, a leading figure of those times who moved in important political circles, had devised his own magical system adapted from the Chaldean structure. An account of Proclus given in *The Sirius Mystery* by Robert K. G. Temple (Destiny Books, VT, 1998) states that 'according to his own claim he could conjure up luminous phantoms of Hekate'—and he was probably the first individual recorded in ancient history to have done so. His actions put him increasingly at odds with the Chaldean imperial policy of the period. Temple goes on to say: 'The connection with the mysteries of Hekate as well as Proclus's practising Egyptian and Chaldean mysteries immediately arouses in the alert reader the suspicion that Proclus might just possibly have known something of the Sirius mystery.' Hekate is a degenerate form of Sirius, according to Temple. Hekate's earliest traditions portray the goddess as having solar rather than lunar origins. Proclus notes that the Chaldeans used astrological symbolism in their rituals. In her highest state Hekate was a member of the Chaldean supreme triad, but her appearance remained truly terrifying as a fully armed triple divinity surrounded by snakes amid fire and burning torches.

Other accounts show Hekate being flanked by lions or 'lion-possessing', which associated her with the zodiacal sign of Leo. In ancient lore one of Hekate's special festivals falls on August 13. The Chaldeans also identified Hekate with other goddesses: Kore, Persephone and Artemis. They believed that Hekate was not just a deity that could be used for invoking forces but that she was the very life force itself, thus giving her a dual aspect; she was a force that had either positive or negative consequences, dictated by the magical operators attempting to harness and direct it. In the wrong hands, this would become a deadly and destructive mental weapon, affecting all who came into contact with it.

The Cosmic Force

During the early 1980s I came to realize that if I and my fellow researchers were going to proceed any further with our attempts to probe into the murky magic of the Hekate group, we would need to know more about what we were dealing with.

Conventional methods of investigation could turn up only so much information in a case such as this. There would always be limits. Magic and the occult are, in themselves, a difficult area in which to pursue any fact-finding mission. But to endeavour to scrutinize a malevolent order such as the Friends of Hekate would present monumental problems—not to mention possible threats to personal safety. Any attempt to infiltrate the group personally and to relay information to outsiders would be akin to signing one's own death warrant. There had to be another way.

Unconventional subject material often requires an unconventional approach if any result is to be achieved. I therefore began to conduct a series of interviews with a very knowledgeable elderly psychic consultant named Mary, who had been personally recommended to me.

Mary had previously been involved in exorcism work in London and the Thames Valley area, and she had visited many ancient and sanctified sites throughout Britain, including Clapham Woods. She had therefore amassed a greater knowledge of the occult than most, and she was able to embrace both the psychic and practical aspects and be cognizant of the implications. She was indeed able to enlarge on what I and my associates already knew and to confirm many of our suspicions.

The older woman at the centre of the Friends of Hekate had apparently been the original 'organizer', according to Mary. The group had been gathering momentum during the 1960s and 1970s. They had a 'proving ground', Mary said, 'so many people had come in, so many had been rejected and gone out on their own.' This process had, of course, enabled the Friends of Hekate to cream off only the most suitable participants for further succession in the Power Spiral. By the mid 1980s they had become 'devilishly organized', Mary believed. She maintained that they were now able to direct their projections of the force in a more concentrated manner, whereas in the past they had been rather ragged in this respect. 'But they are only picking up on the vibrations from the old site', she declared.

She also warned that 'if anyone were to witness a manifestation completely, the power would be conducted to them with a devastating result'. She continued: 'the ground and the very soil itself have become impregnated in some spots as a direct cause of the rituals that have taken place there [Clapham Woods]. The force is strong at certain times during certain periods or hours, or all the time if you happen to be open to certain influences, and all the time to any animal because their instincts are much higher than ours. But as soon as there are too many incidents like the disappearing dogs, then they [the Friends of Hekate] will withdraw and direct the power elsewhere.'

In his classic book *The Devil and all his Works* (1971), Dennis Wheatley defines the force and its uses as follows: 'I have set forth the case for the belief that human beings have a sixth sense, that their minds are capable of both transmitting and receiving impulses for which there is no normal explanation, and that some of the impulses received emanate from the disembodied powers of good and evil.

'Since every process in the Universe of which we are aware is governed by immutable laws, it follows that occult phenomena must also be subject to laws, and that anyone who knows these should be able to make use of them.

'That this has been done in the past is claimed by many occultists in their writings and that it is still being done is claimed by modern magicians. In fact the borderline between magic and science often appears very thin and it is constantly decreasing.'

Wheatley goes on to say: 'We may, therefore, define magic as the application of scientific laws, which are still unknown to our recognized scientists. The putting into force of these occult laws may be likened to a man's having a means by which he can tap in on invisible electric cables and, by them, transmit his will to achieve a desired end.'

Mary had contended that the 'desired end' of the Friends of Hekate was to acquire total occult power. They intended to achieve this by creating a mental war of attrition—a gradual process designed to bleed the natural energies from society and the environment as a whole. If indeed the Friends of Hekate had been able to invoke manifestations from the sub-ethereal plane, it seems highly likely that the UFOs and beams of light witnessed by so many different people were in fact emanations from the ritual experiments being conducted by the group, which were 'sparking off' like electrical discharges during their supposedly 'ragged' period. This notion is shared by Mary and other occult experts I have since spoken to.

As the group progressed and their rituals became deeper, our knowledge of the Friends of Hekate's hierarchical structure indicated that they would be well on their way to achieving their goal as we advanced towards the turn of the millennium.

The Old Worship

We are already aware that the Friends of Hekate were an incongruous order with a malignant strain, and Mary was able to add more to this by providing details of their apparent modus operandi and the history of this vein of worship.

Hekate is normally associated with the Moon, but occult historians have uncovered evidence to suggest that the goddess's origins were more solar than lunar. Mary confirmed this by saying that 'although this is Moon worship they [the Friends of Hekate] don't even work with the Moon—they work with the stars. You know that there are meetings when Orion and the

Archer are showing in the sky, but here there also has to be a conjunction between the planets or their corresponding zodiacal signs—it's all linked to the astrology and astronomy as well as the phases of the Moon. This is why the meetings fluctuate and the dates can swing either side of the customary times by quite a margin, if necessary.

'They don't normally even use Hallowe'en, as that is child's play to them; however, it [their main ritual] has been done on that night as it is good cover and they can appropriate the psychic energies that are about on that night or the following night, as there are two nights here which relate to All Souls and the Festival of the Dead.'

These dates are, of course, October 31, Samhain Eve, and November 1, which is actually the Samhain Festival of the Dead. These festivals are part of pagan lore and are not evil in themselves—no festival is. However, they can be vilified by an order such as the Friends of Hekate, as Mary had suggested.

In her lunar aspect Hekate is worshipped during the waning Moon on 25, 26 and 27 of the Moon—and in the Ancient Greek tradition on the last days of the month. Mary had spoken about those at the heart of the Hekate group. She said, 'The real brains behind it all are five persons, and they come from London, Winchester and Avebury, as you know. Winchester is important,' she continued, 'because you have a centre there, although they don't use it as they do at Clapham. Winchester was the old capital because you are getting right down to the spokes of the Roman wheel.' These were straight lines, which spread out from the centre or hub, which was Winchester.

Mary further disclosed that these locations along with the great white horses etched into the Downs at Oxfordshire and Wiltshire, were all 'on the ring'—an indication that these ancient sites of magical potency were linked by some secret circular configuration.

These sites, though, would be too open for the likes of the Friends of Hekate to conduct any rituals, and Mary confirmed as much. 'Avebury is important for atmosphere but not for meetings as it [their ritual] would be too evident there. They have used the Chanctonbury Ring/Wiston area but its not quite right for them because it doesn't have the same magnetic quality like Clapham, so they cannot build up the vibrations as they would like to. At Clapham you have a strong French connection with the old names. You have more of the old condition, of the Old Worship here. The old Laud comes to rule. You go back to the times before the sea came up, then flooded, and finally receded to its present level.'

Looking at some of the maps showing the estimated shoreline of the British Isles before it became separated in stages from the Continent, it was noticeable that the area to the south of Seaford in East Sussex was probably the last to remain joined to France along the Southern Coast, *c.* 8000 BC.

Occult historian Lewis Spence's work *The Mysteries of Britain* (1925) draws similar conclusions to Mary about Britain's occult history. Spence's contention is that in the British Isles there existed a mystical tradition that was as ancient as the Egyptian and Eastern mysteries but which did not originate directly from them.

According to Spence, Britain owes much of its historical occult lore— not to the Celts but to Iberian elements dating back to the Old and New Stone Age times. These elements involved the religious and esoteric doctrines of the earlier race of Iberians, which Spence maintained had a profound and lasting effect throughout central Europe and particularly on British religious and mystical ideas; the Celts seem to have embodied the Iberian concepts and used them as a basis for their own traditions.

Who were these Iberians, and where did they come from? The Mediterranean, probably north-western Africa where a mysterious religion called the Cult of the Cabiri originated from. These people travelled to Britain in dugout canoes. There is little doubt that they were the old civilized race of the West. Cicero called them the 'Sons of Proserpine' who was goddess of the underworld to many. Others referred to them as the 'Penates of the Romans', meaning the dead presiding as household familiars.

Strabo, the first-century Greek historian and geographer, regarded the Cabiri as 'ministers of Hekate'. Spence sums up the Cabiri as follows:

'This Cabirian cult, then, hailing from north-west Africa, is evidently nothing but a dim survival of memorial of the ancient civilized race of that region, which made its way into Spain, and after undergoing many phases there from Palaeolithic to Neolithic times, gradually found its way, or sent its doctrine of the Cult of the Dead, to Egypt on the one hand and to Britain on the other. This theory explains in a word all the notions of Egyptian influence in Britain, and the many apparent resemblances between Egyptian and British mysticism and folk belief.'

Most ancient sites in Western Europe actually predate the Egyptian ones, according to Spence. He continues his theories on ancient rites by saying:

'Some of the rites and customs of the early Iberian peoples of Britain are still to be found in their pristine entirety among their Iberian kindred in north-west Africa. That the entire rite of Beltane, a rite adopted from the British Iberians by the Celts, should survive in Morocco is, perhaps, the best proof not only of the Iberian origin of druidism, but of the fact that an Iberian people actually brought it to our island.'

According to Spence there were chief seats of worship which belonged to the Cabiri at Lemnos, Boetia, Thessalia and Samothrace. It was at the

latter where the veneration of the Cabiri was said to be at its most potent.

In his *Encyclopedia of the Occult* (1994), Spence quotes from T. D. Kendrick:

'It was in Samothracia that the cult of the Cabiri attained its widest significance, and in this island as early as the fifth century BC their mysteries were held with great éclat and attracted almost universal attention.'

It was also at Samothrace where the cult of the Cabiri amalgamated with that of Hekate. Strabo, who had written about this link, wrote also: 'They say that there is an island near Britain where Demeter and Kore are worshipped with rites similar to the orgies of Samothrace.'

In Egypt, before Herodotus, author T. D. Kendrick states, 'The worship of the Cabiri furnishes the key to the foundation of Rome and the War of Troy itself, as well as the Argonautic expedition. Samothrace and Troad were so closely connected in this worship that it is difficult to judge in which of the two it originated, and the gods of Lavinium, the supposed colony from Troy, were Samothracian'. He concludes that 'the essential part of the War of Troy originated in the desire to connect together and explain the traces of an ancient religion.'

One translation of the name Cabiri is that it contains the two elements of fire and wind, and derives from the Phoenician for 'mighty'.

The legend of Hekate, according to Liz Greene (*The Astrology of Fate*, 1984), can be traced back to her conception of virtually the beginning of time and the creation of the world itself. But Hekate, as far as I am aware, did not appear on the ancient religious scene as a venerated icon until a much later period (*c.* 600 BC), so was I looking at a much earlier, deep-rooted vein of worship?

Chapter 3

The Covert Cult

Diana's Dark Side

Down the ages Hekate has always been identified as a triple-faceted or
three-headed goddess. As occult historian Fred Gettings readily points out
in his book *Dictionary of Demons* (1988), 'The nature of the three heads
changes from tradition to tradition, yet each reflects aspects of the demonic
nature which has made Hekate the tutelary demon of witchcraft,
enchantment and magic.'

Witchcraft and its darker aspects have fuelled one of the longest running
and most fascinating debates in history, with theologians, occult writers,
historians, witches and priests expounding varying viewpoints on the
subject.

But besides the positive and healing attributes being practised by those
involved in what is currently perceived as forms of paganism or New Age,
was there another older and darker worship, which could be interpreted as
the 'older condition of the Old Worship' of which Mary had spoken?

In 1921 one of the most important books of its time, *The Witch Cult of
Western Europe*, was published. Its author, Dr Margaret Murray, an eminent
anthropologist and Egyptologist, had arrived at the conclusion that an
apparently new sect of devil-worshipping witches in fact belonged to an
ancient fertility cult that had existed in Europe for centuries before the
advent of Christianity. The spread of Christianity had driven the witch cult
underground, where it had stayed and secretly thrived for countless
generations, its secret rituals clearly rooted in forms of ancient worship and
handed down to new initiates throughout the ages.

Some devout Christians continued to practise both areas of worship,
reverting in secret to the older rites at certain times of the year.

In the Venerable Bede's *Historica Ecclesiastica Gentis Anglorum* (ed.

C. Plummer, 1896) an account is recorded that in the seventh century King Redwald of the East Saxons maintained two altars in the same temple, one for Christian worship and another smaller one for sacrifice to pagan gods.

Dr Murray remained convinced of the continued existence of such a witch cult, consisting of local groups containing participants drawn from all spheres of society—from the monarch downwards. Being that this secret sect had predated Christianity, it could hardly be referred to as heretic or blasphemous. Its age-old rites were part of a religious order that was completely autonomous from the Church in every way. According to Dr Murray this was a 'Dianic' cult—a group or series of groups who worshipped Diana; this was, apparently, the ancient religion of Western Europe.

Diana, the Roman equivalent of the Moon Goddess, is also linked to Hekate and Artemis. Like that of Hekate, Diana's conception can be traced back to the start of time itself. In her book *An ABC of Witchcraft* (1973), author Doreen Valiente quotes a passage from the doctrine of the Vangelo delle Streghe, which reads: 'Diana was the first created before all creation: in her were all things; out of herself, the first darkness, she divided herself into darkness and light, she was divided. Lucifer, her brother and son, herself and her other half, was the light'.

The Murray theory is given further credence by a collection of witchcraft doctrines published in 1899 called 'Aradia, or the Gospel of the Witches'. In it author Charles Leland uses material taken from an incomplete manuscript written in Italian and translated into English by himself. It sets forth the doctrines of 'La Vecchia Religione', the Old Religion of Witchcraft, and provides evidence for its survival as a religion until the late 19th century. Leland says of Diana, 'Lucifer, or light, lay hidden in the darkness of Diana as heat is hidden in ice'.

Leland asserts that through clandestine religion witchcraft survived. It was not, as the Catholic Church stated, the invocation of Satan, but a much older worship—the cult of the Moon Goddess. Dr Murray divides this into two distinct factions: operative witchcraft and ritual witchcraft. The former she categorizes as involving the use of charms, spells and such like, the latter as a religious order conducting ceremonies based on particular beliefs.

Other authors recognized that the Cult of the Moon Goddess also had two sides, the right- and left-hand paths—the latter, dark side usually associated with Hekate. Diana and Hekate became synonymous, though Hekate was always seen as the blacker of the two.

As Richard Cavendish tells us in his best-selling book *The Black Arts* (1969), 'Hekate was the goddess most often invoked by witches and

magicians. Her triple aspect linked with the Moon's phases, new, full and old, and became identified as Luna, the Moon in the sky, Diana on Earth, and Proserpine in the underworld. She ruled ghosts, night and darkness, tombs, dogs, blood and terror'.

The Ancient Greeks and Romans associated witches with darkness and death. Excesses of power, abuse of knowledge and ruthless personal ambition had often led amoral neophytes onto the left-hand path. According to Theodor Mommsen's *History of Rome* (n. d.) as early as 560 BC the Romans had discovered an 'occult association', a school of black magic of the most revolting kind that celebrated mysteries brought from Etruria (North Western Italy), which had soon spread all over the country. More than 7000 people were charged and prosecuted, and most suffered the fate of execution. Later on, Titus-Livius tells of another 3000 initiates sentenced during a one-year period for the crime of poisoning.

The origins of Diana's name as a goddess and her links with witchcraft can be traced back before biblical times, although the Bible itself links Diana with the ultimate fate of John the Baptist.

In Matthew 14 and Mark 6, the story is told of John the Baptist's last days. King Herod had married Herodias, his brother Philip's wife—a union that John had declared as unlawful. Herodias wanted John killed, but Herod had bound him in prison. When Herod's birthday came around, he celebrated in style with a feast to his lords, high captains and chief estates of Galilee. When the daughter of Herodias danced before Herod, the King was so pleased with her that he swore on oath to grant her anything that she wanted. Under strict instruction from her mother, she asked for the head of John the Baptist—in a charger (plate). Reluctantly the king kept his pledge, and John the Baptist was executed.

Writing about this, Bishop Burchard notes that the goddess Diana was also called Herodias. In some later versions of the *Canon Episcopi*, an important document in the history of witchcraft first published by Regino (*c.* AD 906), the name of Herodias is again linked to that of Diana. Combining these two names can produce Herodiana—which became another name for the goddess Diana during the Middle Ages. Her mythical witch daughter was also called Herodias.

Occult historian Dr W. B. Crow, however, declares that the reverse is true. In his book *A History of Magic, Witchcraft and Occultism* (1968) Dr Crow alleges that Herodias's daughter who danced before King Herod was called Herodiana. Yet all other references to the murder of John the Baptist name her as Salome, whose dance of treachery became known as the 'dance of the seven veils'.

Perhaps Dr Crow had discovered that Salome was also known as

Herodiana because her own mother was named after the same witch legend. He also points out that like Herodiana, some witches indulged in dancing for evil purposes.

Of course, the occult and its practices have a dualistic nature, and there are many practitioners of Dianic worship who are not in any sense evil. However, the origins of the dance of the seven veils can be traced back to the Babylonian fertility goddess Ishtar, who willingly descended into Aralu (the Babylonian Underworld) to retrieve her lover Tammuz. At each of the seven gates of Hell, Ishtar conducts rituals and removes a veil and an item of clothing until she stands naked before the Underworld god. The dance of the seven veils has, therefore, a religious rather than a sensual significance.

During the early Christian period mention of Hekate appears to cease altogether; even so, some continuation of her vein of worship occurs in the form of Diana. In the sixth century AD St Caesarius of Arles expelled from a 'possessed' young girl 'the demon whom the peasants called Diana'.

The following piece is an extract from the *Canon Episcopi*:

> 'It is also not to be omitted that some wicked women perverted by the devil, seduced by illusions and phantasms of demons, believe and profess themselves, in the hours of night, to ride upon certain beasts with Diana, the goddess of pagans, and an innumerable multitude of women, and in the silence of the dead of night, to traverse great spaces of earth, and to obey her commands as of their mistress, and to be summoned to her service on certain nights.'

This is a clear description, albeit in a somewhat muted form, of the Wild Hunt—an ancient legend usually associated with Hekate. Diana came in various forms and assumed multifarious names, adored as a cult goddess throughout the ancient Roman Empire.

The Dianic cult was also significant in ancient Britain. Prince Brutus, who was forced to seek sanctuary there after the fall of Troy, formed the royal line of Britain. Legend has it that it was Diana who led him to Britain. In reciprocation for his kingdom, Brutus, a partly mythical figure and reputed founder of London, was said to have raised a temple to Diana in the form of an altar stone. This became the sanctified relic of London upon whose safety the city is supposed to depend.

A fragment of the original stone is protected behind ornamental iron bars set into the wall of the Bank of China near St Swithin's Lane. In his book *A Guide to Occult Britain* (1976), John Wilcock comments, 'The stone is obviously of prehistoric derivation and must once have marked an important ritual site'. (It has, though, been moved three times in recent centuries.)

Another important ritual site where Brutus founded the main temple of Diana is believed to be where St Paul's Cathedral now stands. During Roman times, oxen were regularly sacrificed there. When excavation work was carried out in the 14th century to lay the foundations for a chapel, more than a hundred scalps of oxen were dug up. The ancient ritual also continued in a christianized form.

In 1375 Sir William Baud was allotted some twenty acres of land belonging to the cathedral site on condition that he supplied the annual sacrifice of horned beasts of Diana. The animals were brought into the old Norman church while the procession was taking place and were offered at the high altar; this church was destroyed in the Great Fire of 1666, and St Paul's Cathedral built in its place.

It was at St Paul's in 1981 that HRH The Prince of Wales and Lady Diana Spencer were married, breaking with a royal tradition that had previously seen such occasions take place at Westminster Abbey. The future monarch's marriage was to prove a disastrous union, ending in a much-publicized separation and divorce.

Then on August 31, 1997 came news that Diana, Princess of Wales, had been killed in a car accident in Paris; the news shook the world. Less than fifteen minutes after news of her death broke over the Internet, the first so-called 'Diana conspiracy' website was inaugurated. During early 1998 conspiracy theories continued to surface in the national press. *The Times* published an article on St Valentine's Day headlined 'Diana: was it murder?', which looked at the various theories being put forward. The exact truth surrounding her death may never be fully known.

The venue for her marriage to the Prince of Wales at the ancient London site was supposed to help bring good fortune. But the former Temple of Diana had shown only her darkest side to her young namesake, in the most tragic manner.

Mary had also said during one of our interviews that there were other places in London that related to the 'spokes of the wheel', one of which petered out at Streatham Common in South London. She referred to this as part of the 'old Steine' (stone circle)—an indication that there was once a stone circle or similar stone configuration in the vicinity of Streatham Common.

She had also spoken previously about Roman roads being laid down upon the 'old spokes of the wheel'—the power lines of ancient Britain—as well as about the need to look for answers way back in history, in the old legends. One such legend concerns the belief that some Roman roads were fashioned by the Devil.

The Dark Worship

The London to Silchester road in Hampshire was historically known as 'the Devil's highway'. It might simply have been that some of the peasants who travelled along it could not imagine how such early engineering feats might be attributed to men alone. But could there be another reason? If Mary was correct and some of the Roman roads had been built on top of an ancient arcane grid system, previously used by early occult priests and sorcerers, this might also have accounted for the nickname.

The original London stone, now seen to have a deeper occult significance, was said by archaeologists to be a 'milestone' from which the Romans measured distances along their network of roads. Certainly Caesar was well aware of the magical potency of the pre-Christian cults in Britain. He said of the druids that they were 'concerned with Divine worship, the due performance of sacrifices public and private, and the interpretation of ritual questions.' He also lamented that they would never commit to writing their secret doctrines about the 'nature of things'.

Lewis Spence sums up the history of witchcraft, its probable origins and links with druidism as follows:

> 'Although we do not hear a great deal about it in British history, there is no doubt that witchcraft, as a more or less secret cult, persisted in Britain throughout the ages, but I do not believe it to have been part of druidism or of the Secret Tradition. Rather it was a debased remnant of that still older Iberian magic which to some extent druidism embraced, but which it also superseded and perhaps tried to weed out. For these and other reasons, I do not think that the witch cult had any connection, official or otherwise, with that of druidism or the Secret Tradition. But it seems to me extremely probable that it borrowed much from the cult of the Secret Tradition, especially as regards some of its ritual practices, which it would debase and turn to evil uses.'

It is assumed that Spence's use of the word 'witchcraft' here refers to the darker and so-called blacker Hekate aspects of the witch cult rather than the more general practices of the 'Old Religion'.

I was able to find another piece of old folklore that relates to this worship in Ralph Whitlock's guide to British folklore, *In Search of Lost Gods* (1979). The author comments: 'the association of the Moon with mental aberrations (lunacy) is extremely ancient and seems to have some basis in fact.'

This would seem to refer to the intensity of the worship and misuse of ritual practices combining to effect and influence certain vulnerable persons. These definitions were as close as I was going to get to the 'old condition of the Old Worship', a forceful weapon if administered by people with malign intent.

The First Incantations

In the beginning religion and magic were both associated with the same conviction that unseen forces of considerable power existed both above the natural plane and as part of the earth. With the passing of time religion and magic seem to have become somewhat estranged, a gradual process that has continued virtually to the present.

The source of the first magic was said to be found on the lost island of Atlantis. Though there is little real evidence left that Atlantis existed, occultists remain convinced that this mythical place flourished as the flagship of the ancient world, before the Dark Worship practised by its own sorcerers brought about its apocalyptic destruction. This event was referred to in the Bible as the Flood.

The Atlanteans had reached an advanced state of evolution, acquiring an immense knowledge of psychic powers. But they continued to abuse their wisdom, which resulted in the initiates engaging in a battle of supernatural supremacy—in effect, the first confrontation between the Sons of Darkness and Sons of Light.

The Egyptian author and magician Rollo Ahmed says as much in his book *The Black Art* *(op. cit.).* Of the Atlanteans he comments, 'They are supposed to have reached an even higher standard of civilization than Man has since attained, but they became adepts of the black art and controlled psychic and elemental forces to dominate the animal and mineral kingdoms. This race is symbolized in the Bible as the Tower of Babel, a civilization whose base rests on earth and whose summit reached into higher realms than man was yet entitled to penetrate.'

Some believe that the Easter Island relics are mysterious memorials to the Atlantean giants, though they were built later. Others say that when the Atlantean sorcerers were expunged, the great Aryan mystics prepared diverse apologues in which they concealed the mysteries. These were known only to a select number of adepts, who were aware of the secrets of what was later referred to as 'witchcraft and sorcery'. Many occultists maintain that this knowledge of witchcraft and of the methods employed by its practitioners is as old as the world itself and has been in use since the days of Atlantis.

The system of hiding the mysteries in the form of clandestine parables was employed by the masters of the ancient world, none of whom wrote the secret knowledge down in a manner that could be easily decoded; they

realized that they were in possession of a mighty double-edged weapon which could not be allowed to fall into the hands of those who would utilize and corrupt its considerable power.

Such was the case with the great Zoroaster, founder of the Magian religion, which started in ancient Persia. The objective of the first teachings of Zoroaster was unity through the triumph of good over evil. But this was soon reversed, as Rollo Ahmed tells us: 'as the years rolled on it degenerated into an idolatrous form of fire worship and its priests were certainly black magicians, judging by the methods employed for divination and the like.'

Taking into account the story of the Atlantean priests, some occult commentators might well point out that this was one aspect of ancient history repeating itself prior to the coming of Christ.

The Horns and the Moon

'The reversal of the signs is being practised here and they [Friends of Hekate] are going into this very deeply. Part of their paraphernalia are the horns, which are linked to the moon', Mary had said.

The images of the Horned God and the Naked Goddess are the oldest surviving icons of worship. One of the earliest examples of the Horned God can be found at the Caverne des Trois Frères in Ariège, France. This is the famous 'Sorcerer', a Stone Age drawing depicting a man covered in an animal's skin and tail, and wearing a face mask. The picture conveys movement, and on top of the dancing man's head are the antlers of a stag.

The association of the horned figure with magic goes right back to the times of the hunter-gatherers who travelled in tribes in search of animal herds. The Horned God, essentially the masculine side of the old lore, is also identified with the leader of the Wild Hunt—the particularly ancient legend associated with Hekate.

In England, the leader is horned: a figure called Herne the Hunter, who was linked to the Celtic Cernunnos, the old Ruler of the Underworld—who also wore horns or antlers. The earliest depictions of Cernunnos that have so far been discovered are the 'Wizard' of Les Trois Frères, Ariège, France, and the Stag Man God from La Pileta, Spain, both of which have been dated to *c.* 13,000 BC.

In Britain one version of the Wild Hunt legend describes Herne the Hunter's search for the King Stag. Accompanied by his infernal hounds, he begins shortly after the summer solstice to track the King Stag, eventually finding and killing him as the autumn equinox approaches. Herne takes the stag's antlers and places them upon his own head. The stag's demeanour and power are transferred to Herne as he takes on the identity of Cernunnos the Stag God.

In Celtic art a serpent with a ram's head represents Cernunnos. The ram is, of course, symbolic of Aries, the sign that begins at the spring equinox. The twisting serpent relates to Scorpio, though that is not the image usually associated with this mystical sign—the serpent's sting or tail is said to represent the mythical fall of Man.

Scorpio rules the House of Death and the old festivals of the dead—Samhain falls during the period of that sign. The serpent is often connected with the Devil. According to the theories of Dr Margaret Murray, the Devil also appeared as a goat and in other animal forms because he was the pagan Horned God of Western Europe. In some parts of Northern and Western Europe it was Cernunnos who was sometimes aspected with triple features similar to that of Hekate.

In her book *An ABC of Witchcraft Past and Present* (*op. cit.*) Doreen Valiente says, 'The horned and hoofed 'devil' of the witches coven has a strong resemblance to the Greek god Pan, worshipped with orgiastic rites by the witches of Thessaly'. Pan was seen as a half-man, half-goat figure whose cult spread throughout the Ancient Grecian world. But it was the horned Greek god Dionysus who was most identified with the goat, though he also appeared as a bull. The Dionysus cult began in the village of Elevtherai, where he was known as Melanaigis—'he with the black goatskin'. Here there was a battle ritually contested between the 'Black One' and the 'Light One'.

Veneration of Dionysus spread to other regions, and at Delphi his cult was associated with the black or midnight sun, and dominated the winter months. However, the image most closely linked to Dionysus is that of the 'Sabbatic Goat' or 'Baphomet of Mendes'. This compounded the Baphomet said to be worshipped by the accursed Knights Templar with the Devil card, number fifteen in the ancient tarot pack, in one image.

This portrayal first appeared in a book called *The Doctrine and Ritual of High Magic* written by the 19th-century French occultist Eliphas Levi. Though this in itself is not necessarily an evil image, the goat icon, which originated in Ancient Egypt, had come to represent a form of the beast, and in the Levi illustration it is the satanic goat of the witches' Sabbath. But this is a latter-day interpretation of an old image of adoration.

Enough arguments have been aired concerning the Murray theory of the survival of a particular cult throughout the ages. One thing most critics are in agreement with is the survival of an idea of specific knowledge relating to a particular cult, whether it is of Cernunnos, Dionysus, Diana/Hekate or Pan.

The image of the horned god is generally more about power than either depravity or evil. In the Old Testament there are references to 'the horns of the altar', and in Crete horns were said to mark a sanctified site.

Michelangelo's statue of Moses shows the prophet with small horns emanating from his forehead. This is based on an old legend that when Moses returned from the summit of Mount Sinai after God had spoken to him, he had grown horns upon his head.

One particular book, which was banned in Germany, contained the alleged secret Words of Power, together with the symbols that were used by Moses. It is supposed to give the adept power over evil spirits, but it is a work that apparently stems from the darker side of ceremonial magic.

The Perversion of the Pentagram

There is a discernible difference between ceremonial magic and witchcraft, and the types of people who become involved. In her book *Where Witchcraft Lives* (Aquarian Press, 1962) Doreen Valiente notes:

> 'Ceremonial magic is the kind of magic contained in the grimoires such as 'The Key to Solomon', 'The Grand Grimoire', 'The Grimorium Verum of the Lemegeton' and the sixth and seventh Books of Moses. It is a tradition which derives for the greater part from the Hebrew Cabala, which in its turn is the Secret Tradition of Israel and possibly stems originally from Ancient Egypt in its basic concepts.'

These concepts involve the invocation and control of spirits by using the secret 'Words of Power' known to King Solomon and Moses.

During medieval times and later, academics were well aware that the Jews were in possession of this secret magical knowledge, so by studying Hebrew they were able to discover the arcane secrets and then translate them into Latin.

There are some ideologies that apply both to ceremonial magic and to witchcraft. Ceremonial magic requires solitude and study on a more intellectual level because of its cabalistic complexities. Witchcraft, on the other hand, is rudimentary, relating to old pagan fertility cults, and can be practised by people who are barely literate but who nonetheless have a feeling for group activities involving the secret use of natural energies.

The modern-day Friends of Hekate, it seemed, were able to combine the two while adhering basically to their own interpretation of the 'Old Religion'. It is likely that their members were drawn from all spheres of society, and Mary demonstrated as much. 'They [the Friends of Hekate] will have come from the man in the street, to the beggar, right up to the aristocracy—if the mind is suitable. They play upon people's fears, indiscretions, desires and their credulity. Once the mind and spirit are broken, you then have total control. They are also adept at acquiring information and influencing people by mentally working on them. They're very clever in this respect.'

I then asked Mary what type of circle the Friends of Hekate used. 'They don't use a circle—they use the pentagram,' she replied. 'It is constructed out of white thread,' she continued.

The pentagram, or five-pointed star, features quite prominently in Christian times. The outstretched human body characterizes the symbol, with the two legs as the lower points, the arms as the mid points, the chest, neck and finally the head as the upper apex, and it is generally regarded as a good or positive image. In fact, the five-pointed star was adopted as an emblem by both superpowers (the USA and the former USSR) as well as Islam. It is also deemed to be a magical symbol, as its points delineate the four fundamentals of life plus the fifth point, which relates to the origins of occult power and should therefore be drawn with one spike in an upwards direction.

But if the pentagram, or 'pentacle', becomes inverted, as in the satanic sciences, it becomes a symbol of malignity feared by practitioners of more pure occult doctrines, who refer to it as the unlucky star (*la mauvaise étoile*). It is seen as containing the image of a goat's head, with the two horns spread into the top two triangles, the forehead and eyes as the centre, the ears as the mid-point and the chin and beard forming the bottom spike. As Doreen Valiente points out, 'In this sense it is the face of the Horned God'.

In 1888 Madame Blavatsky, co-founder of the Theosophical Society, published a book called *The Secret Doctrine*. In it she affirms that the inverted pentagram is the symbol of Kali Yuga, the Dark Age in which we live. There is some conjecture amongst occultists and analysts as to the exact period of time covered by the Dark Age of Kali Yuga. Mme Blavatsky claims that this age lasts 5000 years and that it began in 3102 BC, ending just prior to the turn of the last century, in 1898. The Hindus also claim that Kali Yuga's Dark Age began in 3102 BC with the death of Krishna, but because of the complex manner in which each Yuga (world age) is worked out their tradition insists that the world is still in Kali Yuga's Dark Age. There are some schools of thought based on the Ancient Wisdom that point to the pentagram of Kali Yuga as a symbol that was used by the primeval sorcerers.

The Jews were well aware of sorcery and certain malevolent evocations but apparently knew little of real divine magic. However, their great prophets such as Daniel and Ezekiel did know. The original Ancient Wisdom was said to involve a series of seven keys by which the Ancient Masters

could unlock the door to the ultimate occult Arcana—the seven mysteries of Nature. It was a mysterious language, partly a system of exact science and geometry. It also embodied astronomical, astrological and numerical aspects. The specific knowledge relating to the astrological aspects of the constellations, which were embraced in this method, gave the operator the most extensive capability to carry out 'great' magical feats. It was considered to be of divine derivation and revelation—the very highest form of power.

Some of the secrets of the Ancient Wisdom were undoubtedly contained in the Ark of the Covenant, the exact whereabouts of which continues to baffle academics.

The primordial Hierophants together with the Egyptian High Priests were, at one time, the keepers of the seven keys to the arcane knowledge. But after the fall of Memphis, Egypt began to lose the keys one after the other. The ancient Chaldeans had only three of them in their possession during the time of Berosus, a Babylonian priest of Bel who taught occultism to an elite gathering of followers until his death in 280 BC.

Gradually the knowledge of the seven sub-systems fragmented and fell into the hands of unscrupulous occultists who, although they held only fragments of the original language, possessed what nonetheless remained a potentially dangerous force—a force that could be used to the detriment of mankind according to the nature of the operators who were using it. They had turned the occultism of divine antiquity into a system of sorcery. Thus had they created what may well have been the initial perversion of the pentagram?

Chapter 4
The Primordial Resurgence

Rider of the Sky

I had asked Mary is she could elaborate further on the significance of Orion to the Friends of Hekate. Was it just that the group preferred to hold more winter meetings—when Orion happened to be strong in the sky, together with the Archer—than at other times of the year? No, they were aware of the mystical aspect of Orion.

'In the olden days he was the rider of the sky; but there are so many things connected with the Moon, like the Pleiades and your seven—it can also be a reversible number, reversible because it can be used for good or ill. Apparently it is in the odd numbers that you get the destruction. Although seven is supposed to be a matter of completion—you have to go right back to the old legends to know why we have the seven deadly sins ... The old history, the old legends are the reins of what is in the hands of the people today,' Mary articulated.

What was so special about Orion and the Pleiades? They are both constellations that comprise seven stars. In Greek mythology Orion was the son of Mother Earth—primarily a hunter; his dog Sirius accompanied him. The Pleiades is one of the earliest names given to the seven daughters of Rhiannon, who in British mythology is the ancient mare goddess symbolized by the great white horses etched into the Downs.

On the sacred British wheel the Mare can be found in the southeast, which, according to one tradition, is also the resting place of the Ancients and is linked to the Pleiades. The white horse carved into the Oxfordshire downland at Uffington, which was described by Mary, the elderly psychic, as being 'on the ring', is now believed to date from a thousand years before the previously accepted date of 100 BC. Because it is shaped rather like a dragon, many historians believe that it was originally intended to represent one: there is an ancient link between horses and dragons, and it is on nearby Dragon Hill that St George was said to have slain his infamous foe. The Uffington Horse/Dragon can be viewed fully only from the air. In *The Ancient British Goddess* (1991), Kathy Jones comments: 'at the time it was constructed there were no aeroplanes. Who is to say that our ancestors were not the seven daughters of Rhiannon who came to Earth from the Pleiades? They may have arrived in fire-breathing vehicles that looked like dragons, bringing with them the knowledge that tamed the wild horses.'

There is, however, another fascinating and disturbing aspect to the idea of alien intelligence, which links together both the Pleiades and Orion, according to one theory.

In his book *The Undiscovered Country* (1976) Stephen Jenkins discusses evidence that beings that originate from Orion are coming to Earth with a view to eventually taking it over. The main evidence for such an extraordinary theory takes the form of messages from—or indeed close encounters with—what contactees say are alien entities who claim to belong to the Pleiades. The Pleiadians were, it is said, posing as our allies, delivering stern warnings of the celestial conflict to come.

It is tempting to dismiss all this as the stuff of TV's *X-Files* storylines, but the author is a trained historian who presents an in-depth hypothesis based for the most part on wide research. Of particular interest is the fact that common ground is shared, in his theories, with the esoteric 'Wheel of Time' Tantric Buddhist teachings.

Knowledge of this, even among Buddhists, is apparently fairly rare. But Stephen Jenkins had found a qualified master who told him about the concept of the metaphysical or spiritual mode of existence. They discussed the possible existence of what the author refers to as 'inter-penetrating levels of being, each occupying this area of space, but each mutually exclusive of all the others'. They also discussed the methods that entities of one universe might employ in order to contact another. This would involve each of the 'levels of being' adopting a physical existence which would be 'beyond the physics of any other'.

This concept, while being impenetrable to most Western minds, is accepted by several Eastern philosophies. In some aspects of Hinduism there is a similar theory that our existing physical universe comprises one quarter physical and three-quarters metaphysical planets.

Jenkins refers to his own teacher as being 'pretty deep in this ocean of abstruse speculation', insisting 'that particular metaphysical planets were located in particular regions of space, in individual constellations'.

Some aspects of Eastern philosophy refer to the unknowable Divine

Being—the Primordial Buddha. A parallel can be found in the 'Tao' of Chinese teaching. But these 'beings' can appear to certain people in the form of the great 'Manifestation' or 'apparitions of aspects of the Divine Power' (Jenkins, *op. cit.*). Jenkins alludes to this as a 'hierarchy of metaphysical beings', expressed in the form of religious images or icons which he says provide a link between the Great Mother, the Tree of Life and the Triple Goddess in the form of Artemis.

There is a feminine predominance in advanced Tantric practice involving two stages. The first embraces a female partner for the male adept, in the accepted sense of a human being. The second encompasses the female as a superior metaphysical power, worshipped by a male adept.

In Tibet the female phantom that is said to frequent parts of north-west India is called *Kardomah* or 'sky-walker'. Another Eastern manifestation of the Great Goddess came in the form of Kali the Black—the female counterpart of Shiva, the destroyer.

The Seat of the Ancient Wisdom

The Wheel of Time is also called *Kalachakra*, and contains elements of Kalachakric practise that are outside the perimeters of what would normally constitute mainstream Buddhism. The Kalachakrian texts emphasize leanings towards astronomy and astrology, dividing the latter into seven branches. In poetical pieces *Kala*, 'time', is seen driving a seven-wheeled chariot with seven reins.

Central to the Wheel of Time philosophy is the conviction that there exists a mystical city or dwelling place known as *Shambhalla*, the land of bliss. This legend features as 'Shangri La' in James Hilton's fictional work *Lost Horizon* (1933). It suggested that the mythical kingdom was located somewhere in the Himalayas, but most other sources place Shambhalla outside Tibet, near the Altaic mountains. Author Geoffrey Ashe (*The Ancient Wisdom*, 1977) indicated that Shambhalla could be part of an even older tradition, which had been conserved as part of the Bon religion that predated Buddhism in Tibet.

The Russian artist, adventurer and psychic Nicholas Roerich accompanied by his anthropologist son George, led an expedition through Central Asia from 1923 to 1928 to try to discover the lost land. In the physical sense his party were unable to achieve their goal; however, Roerich did attain a greater understanding of the Shambalic concept through meeting a learned lama at the end of his travels. But the most unexpected outcome of his Far Eastern explorations was a classic UFO sighting witnessed by seven members of the expedition, including Roerich himself.

The Roerich sighting was well ahead of its time, in view of the UFO mania

that has persisted throughout the last few decades and which continues to confront the sceptics with the sheer volume of sightings—some apparently being accompanied by personal contact with aliens.

The Roerich incident included the precursory appearance of a large black eagle: this prompted the group to look upwards, and they immediately saw a huge, oval-shaped object hurtling across the cloudless sky before disappearing into the distance. The object was shiny and metallic in appearance; in 1927 there was little in the way of modern aerial technology—particularly in Central Asia—that it might have been confused with.

Scholars who have studied the Roerich account have adjudged that there was probably a psycho-interactive factor involved. Roerich had just erected a Shambalic shrine, and he was said to be in a state of 'mystical expectancy', according to author Geoffrey Ashe, who documented the affair in *The Ancient Wisdom*.

The lamas who shared the Roerich apparition referred to it as 'the sign of Shambhalla'. Afterwards, one lama who did not witness their experience nonetheless came to the same conclusion. Roerich's UFO was viewed, therefore, not as an extraterrestrial space craft, but more as psycho-interactive luminosity—a manifestation of a force that was possibly linked somehow to Roerich's frame of mind and concentration of thought at the time.

I recalled some of Mary's words during one of our interviews, when she had referred to the emanations, which can result after a period of uninterrupted fixating by the mind. Though Mary had mentioned this in connection with rituals performed by the Friends of Hekate, given Roerich's surroundings at the time, coupled with his state of mind, it is quite feasible that a similar set of conditions could have applied here.

It is the belief among some scholars of the occult that only in India, China and Tibet can be found men in the present day that still possess knowledge of the complete seven 'sub-systems', which provide the key to the integral system of the hidden mysteries. In his book *Shambhalla, Oasis of Light* (1977), Andrew Tomas looks more closely at the mysteries and their significance in the ancient world. He supports the theory that the secret knowledge was deliberately disguised in the form of an inscrutable language in order to safeguard the Greater Mysteries. He quotes Plato's words in a letter sent to Dionysius the Younger: 'I must write to you in enigma so that if my letter is intercepted by land or sea, he who shall read it may in no degree comprehend it.'

Andrew Tomas quotes the initiates as saying that because of the veiled symbology of the Greater Mysteries, 'their teaching is unintelligible to fools'. Plato is described in some works as being a 'great initiate' himself. But Plato was also aware that the symbols of magic and the occult science have a dual power. Their misuse is fraught with peril, particularly if the experimenter is not being properly guided. There are the right- and left-hand paths. It is said that the key to the symbols can only be given by word of mouth from the adept, though there are in existence several works that provide accounts of higher forms of magic which, if pursued without proper guidance, can pose a real danger to the dabbler.

In Phaedrus, Plato describes man's magical role prior to his descent into the cesspit of sorcery: 'Before Man's spirit sank into sensuality and became embodied through the loss of his wings, he lived among the gods in the airy spiritual world where everything is true and pure.'

In *Shambhalla, Oasis of Light* Andrew Tomas quotes a paragraph from *The Tibetan Book of the Dead* by W. Y. Evans-Wentz: 'Since very early times there has been a secret international symbol-code in common use among the initiates which affords a key to the meaning of such occult doctrines as are still jealously guarded by religious fraternities in India, as in Tibet and in China, Mongolia and Japan.'

Philo Judaeus, the first-century historian, stated that 'the Mysteries were known to unveil the secret operations of Nature.' Proclus was also quoted as saying that 'the gods exhibit many forms of themselves and appear in a variety of shapes, and sometimes indeed a formless light of themselves is held to the view.'

Andrew Tomas believed there was a steady exchange of knowledge between what he terms 'the widely separated groups of initiates in Asia and the Mediterranean basin in spite of the great distances involved'. Certainly the Etruscans brought a mixture of influences with them from Asia Minor and Egypt when they settled in north-west Italy in 900 BC.

Tomas had always considered Nicholas Roerich to be his master ever since their first meeting in Shanghai in 1935. Roerich had several books published at this time while his wife, writing under the name of J. Saint-Hilaire, had one book published in 1930 called *On Eastern Crossroads*. It was in this work that, according to Stephen Jenkins, references were made to the location of Shambhalla being somewhere in Orion itself. Jenkins comments about these references in his own book *The Undiscovered Country* as follows:

'The reported statements of the entities about beings living somewhere
in Orion are a reflection of an actually existing Central Asian tradition,
and the statements of Roerich's offer some confirmation of this, although
they merely connect Orion with an earthly, if mystical, Shambhalla.'

In his book *The Ancient Wisdom*, Geoffrey Ashe cites other examples linking Orion with some form of mystical adoration taken from Roerich's travel

diary, *Altai Hilalaya*, published in 1930. Roerich refers to the mountain Belukha, the principal peak of the Altai range, which he says means 'Orion—dwelling of gods.' Roerich claims that this explanation is comparable with the 'world-mountain of other mythologies'. He also writes: 'the cults which surround some constellations such as the Bear and Orion amaze you by their widespread popularity. The wisdom of the shamans designates them for worship.'

The semi-mythical figure of Gesar, who was believed to have lived in the eighth century AD, is associated with the Orion constellation, according to Roerich; he also links Gesar with Shambhalla. The legend of Gesar-Khan refers to the severed heads of seven blacksmiths, which were sent to Khan-Khan. He created seven chalices out of them, but eventually these were dispersed into the heavens and formed the Great Bear constellation. Roerich also links Gesar-Khan with the seven-starred constellation, while Geoffrey Ashe takes this notion further by saying that it 'could be rooted in a single Altaic concept of the seven stars as seven undifferentiated Wise Ones—smiths, shamans'.

According to Ashe, shamanism was once a female cult, which is related in turn to the Siberian Earth Goddess and the Bear constellations. He hints strongly at a 'Siberian Artemis'. Similar parallels can be drawn here with the feminine predominance in advanced Tantric practice and what Stephen Jenkins refers to as a 'hierarchy of metaphysical beings', expressed in the form of religious icons symbolizing, among others, the Triple Goddess.

Tantric magic involves a belief in the invisible powers of the universe—positive or negative, creative or destructive, controlling the cycle of life and death—which can be utilized by certain magical rituals. While objecting, in principle, to Tantric magic, some scholars of Eastern philosophy and ideas hold the Kalachakra—the secret science that is presumed to be a legacy of Shambhalla—in great esteem.

The belief in the existence of Shambhalla is central to the Wheel of Time of the Kalachakrian system of studies. Nicholas Roerich's son, Dr George Roerich, commented on this in one of his written works as follows: 'The whole question of the Kalachakrian system is closely interwoven with the problem of the realm of Shambhalla, a mystical region from where the Kalachakrian system was brought to India in the second half of the 10th century.'

The final cause of the Kalachakrian practitioners is to locate the kingdom of Shambhalla and partake in a form of religious mass with its leader, according to George Roerich. The ultimate question remains at the heart of the quest for Shambhalla, though. Its precise location continues to remain a subject for debate. The Roeriches thought it to be a heavenly domain occupying a celestial sphere somewhere in Orion. Others believe it lies underground, with subterranean passages—an idea that links it, in theory, to the lost world of Agharti.

Believers in the legend of Agharti accept the existence of an arcane underground kingdom secretly situated in an immense conglomerate of tunnels and caverns somewhere in Asia. Access to this netherworld, and its precise position, are known only to a select group of adepts; the place is said to contain a vast library of occult lore and manuscripts whose origins go back to the days of Atlantis.

The legends of Agharti and Shambhalla are startlingly similar but are not, apparently, the same. The labyrinth of Agharti is supposed to stretch across the world, whereas Shambhalla is confined to a specific location—albeit a differing one, according to the various devotees; some lamas believe it was once located in Celtic Britain at the sanctified site of Glastonbury.

Whatever Shambhalla's true location might be, its nature and purpose are clearly defined in *The Occult Conspiracy* (1989) by Michael Howard, according to whom the lost city was 'the legendary home of a fraternity of occult adepts or masters who had secretly influenced world affairs throughout history.' These people were referred to as the 'Great White Brotherhood', the 'Secret Chiefs' or 'Hidden Masters'. Belief in their existence apparently lay behind the inauguration of such organizations as the freemasons, the Templars, the Theosophical Society and other similarly significant groups.

The Nazis' Secret Quest

The co-founder of the Theosophical Society, Madame H. P. Blavatsky, had written about the possible existence of a concealed kingdom situated somewhere in the East and presided over by Hidden Masters.

In her first book, *Isis Unveiled*, which was published in 1877, she refers to the temple of Asgartha in what is presumed to be Agharti. She also mentions the 'Brahm-Atma'—the master of initiates. The French occultist Saint-Yves d'Alveydre claimed to have been schooled by a Brahmin in the hidden Eastern knowledge. The Brahmin, who had become exiled from his own country and had settled in Le Havre, France, told Saint-Yves that a place called 'Agartha' in central Asia contained massive underground archives referring back aeons in time. It was the centre of initiates presided over by a hierarchy of twelve supreme initiates. Once again the parallels between Agharti and Shambhalla are all too clear.

René Guenon, a writer who was generally against the Theosophical Movement and Mme Blavatsky, asserted that Agharti and Shambhalla were multifarious centres: the Chiefs of the former were involved in meditation while those of the latter were engaged in magical rituals, he believed.

Blavatsky herself had made references to Shambhalla in her later book *The Secret Doctrine*, published in 1888. One passage mentions that the chief of all initiators is associated with a mysterious sacred island in Central Asia, which she later refers to as the 'fabled Shambhalla'.

However, in the years to follow, those with far more sinister motives were to become aware of the magical legends and the prospective powers that could be obtained from the dual centres of Agharti and Shambhalla.

In 1925, the first of several yearly expeditions set out from Munich and headed east, to Tibet. Its target and specific brief was to make contact with the underground adepts of Agarthi and Shambhalla, and to 'persuade them to enlist the aid of Luciferic and Ahrimanic powers in the furtherance of the Nazi cause and in the projected mutation which would herald the new race of supermen.'

This last passage is taken from Trevor Ravenscroft's occult classic *The Spear of Destiny* (1973), an influential and controversial exposé of Hitler's hidden agenda in his quest for total power and domination.

Ravenscroft based his research on the twelve years spent with Dr Walter Johannes Stein, a knowledgeable occultist. Stein was also a special adviser to Sir Winston Churchill on the Führer's thinking, and that of the Nazi hierarchy, behind their actions and their motivations. Churchill himself was adamant that the Nazis' involvement with the occult should remain under wraps—thus Dr Stein was 'leaned on' not to lay open before an unsuspecting public exactly what he knew.

Dr Stein, however, did reveal his authoritative knowledge of the Nazis' secret quest for occult power to Ravenscroft, who was able to publish it in *The Spear of Destiny*.

Once the Nazi expedition had established contact with those Tibetans whom they believed to be the supreme magi from the centres of Agharti and Shambhalla, they were brought back to Berlin, where they lived and became known as 'The Society of Green Men'. Their real reason for being in Germany remained a closely guarded secret. Hitler himself held regular meetings with their leader.

The expedition was largely a product of the ambitions of the sinister Professor Karl Haushofer, one-time German military attaché in Tokyo. Haushofer had travelled widely in the Far East searching for occult information and sometimes finding it in the form of Eastern secret societies, with which he made personal contact. During his stay in Tibet, in 1908, Haushofer met George Ivanovitch Gurdjieff, a Russian occultist credited with having an influence over the German Order.

Gurdjieff had also known Josef Stalin while the future Soviet tyrant was a student, lodging at Gurdjieff's house. Gurdjieff initially made Haushofer aware of the legends surrounding Agarthi and Shambhalla.

According to Trevor Ravenscroft in *The Spear of Destiny* (*op. cit.*), the twin centres were referred to in some pre-Nazi literature. He says that 'The Luciferic Oracle was called Agarthi and believed to be a centre of meditation which concentrated on giving sustenance to the powers. The Ahrimanic was named Shambhalla, a centre where rituals were performed to control elemental powers. The initiates of Agarthi specialized in astral projection and sought to inspire false leadership in all civilizations in the world. The adepts of Shambhalla sought to foster the illusion of materialism and lead all aspects of human activity into the abyss.' Ravenscroft further denigrates the image of the two centres of magic by describing them as 'the twin resonators of evil'.

As we have already discussed, evil does not reside in 'magic' or 'force' per se but in the nature of the operators who are trying to harness their powers. Such was the case with Agarthi and Shambhalla. They were considered to be divine magical centres of the utmost antiquity before the Nazis' interest in them introduced injurious elements, which defiled the legend of the twin centres unfairly but probably for all time.

During the 1920s and 1930s the Nazis also became interested—largely through the ideas of occultists Alfred Rosenberg and Rudolf Steiner—in the Zoroastrian religion, with its dualistic philosophy of the eternal struggle between light and darkness. Rosenberg was acting leader of the National Socialists from 1922 to 1924, and during this period he laid the foundations for the Nazi Party's attempts to revive German paganism as part of their ideology.

Rosenberg was sure that the Aryan race had been created on the lost continent of Atlantis, where many ancient occult ideologies had originated. He also believed that the Atlantean priesthood had been forewarned of the impending destruction of their primordial continent, so they were able to depart quickly and install themselves in the Middle East—including in Persia, where they helped found the Zoroastrian religion. They were also said to have been instrumental in establishing Agharti more than 60,000 years ago.

The sacred perpetual flame of Zoroaster, the spiritual teacher who lived in north-eastern Persia *c.* 600 BC and who first introduced fire as the sole object of worship to the ancients of Persia, was seen as the symbol of light, unity and monotheism (belief in one god). But in the Sassanian period, spanning the second to the seventh centuries AD, Zoroastrianism became the official religion of the Persian Empire and took on a classical form of religious dualism.

This dualism was embodied in the form of Ahura Mazda and his sons— the only gods that were accepted into the teachings of Zoroaster. Ahura

Mazda was amalgamated with his good son Ormazd, who was surrounded in light, while his other son, Ahriman, was evil and dwelt in darkness.

By the time of the Persian Empire's revival under the House of Sassan, however, Ahriman had come to hold unequalled power in his own kingdom of darkness—hence Rollo Ahmed's conclusions that the Zoroastrian priests had degenerated into 'black magicians' (see Chapter 3). This perpetuated the myth of the eternal twin gods, as the question of evil remained at the very heart of Zoroastrianism. Zoroastrians believed that the perpetual struggle between the two gods would end in triumph for Ormazd, who would trample the snake-covered head of his dark brother Ahriman. The beliefs initiated by Zoroaster were represented in certain passages in the Dead Sea Scroll of the Essences.

In *The Devil and All His Works* (1971), Dennis Wheatley, who describes Zoroastrianism as 'one of the great religions of the world' says of its beliefs and influences, 'those beliefs were inherited by the gnostics and later by the alchemists. They played a major part in formulating the conception that every happening in the universe and act of every individual can be attributed to either the power of light or the power of darkness.'

The Nazis, of course, had concentrated their energies on attempting to harness the latter.

According to Trevor Ravenscroft, 'Ahriman' or Ahrimanic spirits had figured quite saliently in some of their early literature—naming the Ahrimanic oracle Shambhalla, for example—as quoted earlier in this chapter. But the Nazis had corrupted all of this for their own malign purposes—and in the end it may well have rebounded upon them, resulting in their final destruction.

Towards the end of the war, when Haushofer fell out of favour with the Nazi hierarchy, the mysterious figure of Friedrich Heilscher—who was not a Nazi Party member—emerged to play a prominent role during the terminal war years. Heilscher was said to be a 'member of a world cult of a higher order', and no less a figure than Heinrich Himmler held him in the highest esteem. Trevor Ravenscroft refers to the 'Ritual of the Stifling Air', which was especially engendered by Heilscher and whereby 'select members of the SS took oaths of irreversible allegiance to satanic powers'.

On April 25, 1945 a group of Russian soldiers sifting through the debris that was once Berlin, discovered the bodies of seven Tibetans wearing German military uniforms, six lying in a circle around the seventh man, whose hands were clasped together and encased in bright green gloves. In the days that followed more Tibetans were found in similar circumstances, all apparently having committed ritual suicide in the same bizarre manner.

There were strong fictional echoes of the Nazis' objectives in acquiring occult power in Stephen Spielberg's modern-day film classic *Raiders of the Lost Ark* (1981). Here, of course, Nazi emissaries travel to remote eastern parts in order to recover an ancient artefact that will reveal the exact whereabouts of the Ark of the Covenant. To date, no one has made a film about Hitler's real quest for occult power.

The Reversible Seven

The right-handed swastika adopted by Adolf Hitler as the Nazis' emblem consists of four interlocking reversed sevens. It was an occultist called Friedrich Krohn who had originally submitted the swastika to Hitler, based on the traditional left-hand design.

The Thule Society emblem of 1919 shows a not dissimilar design of four reversed curved sevens, superimposed with the handle of a sword, which is pointing downwards. The Thule Society, of which Krohn was a prominent member, had taken its name from the mythical hyperborean island believed by occultists to be part of Atlantis and the source of northern occult wisdom.

The Thulists became a very important secret order in Germany. They combined occultism with extreme right-wing politics and had many influential society members. Phenomenal claims were made about their activities. One guest, an occultist called Dietrich Eckhart, organized séances where, it was alleged, ectoplasm emanated from the vagina of the medium and developed into human forms. When in a state of deep trance, the medium often spoke in another language, on one occasion predicting that a Messiah would rise and lead Germany to victory and the domination of the world.

Seven is the magical number that governs magic ceremonies and the mysteries of the occult. It relates to the 'Nature' or 'God' force, and appears often in the Bible in connection with magical powers. The number seven connects both astrology and alchemy, and also unites them mystically in a greater whole.

Mme Blavatsky, too, stresses the significance of seven in *The Secret Doctrine*, presenting it as the supreme number of the higher mysteries. Since pre-Christian times astrologers have used seven (Sun, Moon, Mercury, Venus, Mars, Jupiter and Saturn) as a working basis. Seven is considered to be a sacred number in many societies, including Egyptian, Greek and Hindu. It is also said to rule the rhythms of life. The five planets plus the Sun and the Moon, which formed the ancient system, were all believed to have an influence on events here on Earth. The Moon, our closest celestial neighbour, has the biggest influence on the cycles or rhythms of our lives.

In his book *The Black Arts* (1969) Richard Cavendish states that 'the significance of seven comes from its connection with the Moon. It is a

widespread primitive belief that the cycle of life and death on Earth—the birth, growth and decay of plants, animals and men—is connected with the waxing and waning of the Moon as it goes through its endless cycle of births and deaths in the sky.'

The four phases of the Moon each last seven days. The antiquity of seven, its mysterious importance and deep historical roots are featured almost as a central theme running throughout Geoffrey Ashe's book *The Ancient Wisdom* (*op. cit.*). In it the author traces the number's origins back in time, eventually arriving at a period before 6000 BC in northern Russia.

The association of the north and northern lands with occult power derives from the legend of Hyperborea. In the seventh century BC a Greek priest named Aristeas of Procennesus is believed to have travelled in search of his patron Apollo's Hyperborean home. When he returned to Greece, he recounted his expedition details in the form of a poem called 'Arimmaspea', only fragments of which have survived, being incorporated in the writings of other authors on the subject.

Aristeas, apparently, was never quite able to reach his ultimate destination, but he was able to come into contact with a race of people who called themselves the 'Issedonians', who told him that the Hyperboreans lived near a region rich in gold and guarded by griffins. In this area was the wind Boreas, on the other side of which lived the Hyperboreans.

In *The Ancient Wisdom* Geoffrey Ashe points out that, to an early Greek, the strong, cold Boreas wind would blow from the north—but to a Russian living in Asia it would come from the east. The Hyperboreans were ostensibly situated in a more eastern than northern location, and Ashe is convinced that the 'Land of the Hyperboreans' and Shambhalla are the same legend seen 'through a separate tradition'.

He also produces a considerable quantity of evidence to establish that the grounds for seven as a mystical number lie in the seven stars that comprise the constellation of the Plough/Ursa Major, also known as the Great Bear. Ashe then presents his main hypothesis that the constellation was thus named because early northern man worshipped the bear: 'ursine' or bear cults spanned a great part of the northern hemisphere. Ashe also postulates that bear worship started in Russia *c.* 8000 BC, but Neanderthal Man was making altars out of bear skulls nearly 100,000 years ago, which takes us back to a pre-Ice Age period.

Mary had said that the old condition of the Old Worship 'had gone right back to beyond the time when the sea had come up and flooded much of the land, thus forcing England to be annexed from the rest of what is now Western Europe'. I had taken this to mean that she was referring to some form of pre-Ice Age adoration.

These very early priests or group heads would, in all probability, have assumed the mantle of the animal being worshipped, so at some point during the ritual they could actually 'become' the bear by wearing its skin and head—in the manner that the horned stag and other animal skins were worn by those engaged in similar worship; coven leaders also appeared as animals during witches' rites.

The Great Bear, or Plough, constellation—called the Seven Bears by the early Hindus—is the most conspicuous in the northern Hemisphere. Both the Orion and Pleiades constellations comprise seven stars, as previously mentioned. Orion's brightest neighbouring star is Sirius. However, apart from their obvious connection, these star groups have one other intriguing thing in common: each has been the subject of postulation by three different writers that they are the home of advanced alien intelligence!

Geoffrey Ashe strongly indicates that the knowledge that allowed early man to develop was brought by extraterrestrial visitors from Ursa Major.

In *The Sirius Mystery* Robert K. G. Temple presents the theory that more space travellers—this time from Sirius—were instrumental in providing the Dogon tribe of West Africa with an understanding of modern astronomy that was many centuries ahead of its time. The primitive Dogons worshipped Sirius, conducting complex religious ceremonies which in all probability, dated back several thousand years. Fragments of their practices and convictions spread and found their way into Greco-Egyptian magic and religion. Both Temple and Robert Graves link Sirius to Hekate—albeit in a degenerate form (see Chapter 2).

I have already looked at Stephen Jenkins's ideas concerning alien life-forms or energies that emanate from Orion and Pleiades constellations—one purportedly Earth-hostile, the other Earth-friendly. The notion of celestial conflict is quite a time-worn one. It finds common ground in Christianity, Buddhism and Egyptian Gnosticism. There is, however, one final part to this intriguing saga of alien intervention.

It concerns the particularly peculiar phenomenon of messages discovered on tape recordings—some in Morse code. These referred to in a book called *The Scoriton Mystery* by Eileen Buckle. Stephen Jenkins met and discussed with Eileen Buckle the nature and possible origins of the messages she claimed had appeared on her own tape recorder, one being received on June 18, 1966 at Edburton Hill in Sussex.

The whole matter was so strange that she was reluctant to say too much: there was no clear scientific explanation for it. Stephen Jenkins became utterly convinced of her genuineness the more they conversed. One of the messages was particularly intriguing to Jenkins. It was received on the night of July 10, 1966 and began in Morse code. It spoke of a period in twenty days time when 'Dhanne's in trine'. 'Trine' is an astrological term, which refers to any two points on the circumference of the circle that are 120 degrees apart. Eileen Buckle apparently knew nothing of these terms or names. Nor did her fellow researcher. But to Stephen Jenkins the pronunciation of Dhanne was extremely close to Danae—the Greek goddess who became assimilated into Diana.

On the night of Saturday July 30, 1966, twenty days from the night of the recording, there was just one constellation that was 'in trine' with the full Moon—Pleiades. When Stephen Jenkins asked Eileen Buckle who her entities claimed to be, she told him that she 'thought of them as among those from the Pleiades'.

Many of the messages received were of a particularly unpleasant nature, intoning threats against non-compliers. According to Jenkins, this reversal of attitude could be a propaganda ploy aimed at making us believe that the Pleiadean entities were our allies when the opposite may well be true—in which case we have nothing to fear from the Orion populace, whoever or whatever they may be!

The entirely speculative theories that alien intelligence is the source of the Ancient Wisdom or occult power remain intriguing. Diana is associated with the constellation of Ursa Major, or the Great Bear, as well as being the Moon goddess—thus providing us with a link to Geoffrey Ashe's theory of 'Bear Worship'. Hekate, though, is connected to Sirius, which, looking at the celestial map, forms the base of a diagonal configuration with Orion in the middle and the Pleiades at the top end. This points not only to Hekate but also to Diana as having both solar and lunar traditions.

In his book *Cults of the Shadow* (1975), Kenneth Grant firmly suggests that the origins of sorcery and witchcraft 'were degenerate survivals of a pre-human phase of our planet's history, generally—though mistakenly—classified as Atlantean'. While some authorities are of the opinion that these roots stem from a race of Mongol or Eastern origin, or indeed Atlantis itself, Grant takes the whole concept of where witches came from even further back in time than that: 'They were non-human entities, that is to say they predated the human life-wave on this planet, and their powers—which would today appear unearthly—derived from extra-spatial dimensions. They impregnated the aura of the Earth with the magical seed from which the human foetus was ultimately generated.'

The artist and occultist Austin Spare laid claim to having had some form of contact concerning the existence of alien intelligences—a belief shared by Aleister Crowley, who tried to uphold the notion of an independently existing superhuman consciousness and extraterrestrial entities.

Kenneth Grant also refers to the 'in-betweenness concepts that together compose the eightfold cross, the eight-petalled lotus, a synthetic symbol of the Goddess of the Seven Stars plus her son, Set or Sirius'. The photograph of the demonic mural taken in Clapham village, Sussex, England, shows a figure holding a religious orb with an eight-armed cross and circle. In another passage Grant describes Hekt or Hekate as a transformer from 'the dark and baleful Moon of witchcraft to the full bright orb of magical radiance.'

Many of the theories Grant analyzes in *Cults of the Shadow* have their origins in primeval rituals and customs. Of the witch cult he says, 'The principal symbols of the original cult have survived the passage of aeon-long cycles of time. They were carried over from the Draconian or Typhornian Traditions of pre-dynastic Egypt. They all suggest the Backward Way—the Way of Resurgent Atavisms [a reversion to an ancestral, primitive or primordial type].'

Grant then acknowledges the symbols as, among others, the Sabbath, the number seven, the Moon, forms of a webbed or winged nocturnal creature, and Hekt or Hekate. He sums up the cult as follows: 'These and similar symbols originally typified the Draconian tradition which was degraded by the pseudo witch cults during centuries of Christian persecution. The Mysteries were profaned and the sacred rites were condemned as anti-Christian. The cult thus became the repository of inverted and perverted religious rites and symbols having no inner meaning; mere affirmations of the witches' total commitment to anti-Christian doctrine, whereas originally they were living emblems, sentient symbols of *ante*-Christian faith.'

The knowledge of the Mysteries and the Ancient Wisdom had, in part, been allowed by various corrupt priesthoods to degenerate into the Dark Worship.

The theories of Robert Temple concerning the unique astronomical understanding of the Dogon tribe of Africa and its link to Sirius have impressed both believer and cynic alike. Certainly the rituals of the mysteries would have had to begin somewhere and at some point in time—if not Atlantis, then the East, or possibly Iberia or Africa.

But the burning question remains: who brought such knowledge in the first place, and from where? Could this knowledge conceivably comprise the remnants or fragments of a much earlier legacy left by extraterrestrials, as some have suggested? Mary, the elderly psychic, had always maintained

that the Friends of Hekate were going into all this very deeply, and looking into the origins of the Dark Worship; I had been able to find many links with the old condition of the Old Worship that she had continually spoken of. But how would this knowledge be used by the current order, in particular the incumbents at the very centre?

Chapter 5

The Seventh Seal

The Deadly Sorceress

'The younger woman [the high priestess] is the most dangerous in this set-up,' Mary revealed. 'She is a member of the aristocracy and very well connected. The older woman [the original organizer] is similarly connected. The man [the master] is the medic. These three are the focal points of the group and they are all aware of each other.'

I asked Mary how I could be aware of them if our paths should ever cross in an ordinary, everyday situation. 'You would feel a sudden freezing-up inside yourself, and I don't mean like a frost, but more like a sudden deep cold that goes right through you to your very bones. You would also feel that you wouldn't want to go near that person or touch them.'

Mary, of course, was a strong 'sensitive' in her field, but she was, in effect, saying that I could sense the same things with enough degree of concentration. But what sort of people were we looking at, and how *do* they present themselves in everyday situations?

'You are looking at faceless people,' Mary continued. 'They wear a mask and are able to portray a face of complete normality. They shop at supermarkets; the High Priestess sometimes visits pubs. She is fair, but I wouldn't take too much notice of colouring because that can be changed. The hierarchy possess the ability to blend in with the natural surroundings whenever they wish to do so. If you look at many of your historical and religious figures, the most insignificant-looking are often the most important.'

I asked how often the 'centre' comes down to attend meetings, as we understood that they only attended the important ones.

'The Centre comes down on the four definite times of the year, though

the exact timings can change, as you know. It's a feast day but they have also used another site—a dark little wood where no birds sing. I did visit there once and the atmosphere was awful. It's near Burpham, not far from Arundel. There's a current French connection with this group because I feel as if I want to hop across the Channel ...'

I then questioned Mary about our vulnerability during the course of our on-going investigations.

'Your greatest form of protection is within yourself—in the form of positive thought power, and there is nothing quite like this for defeating their [Friends of Hekate's] application of the force. So, if you do that they cannot touch you,' Mary declared emphatically. 'But you need to go easy on your communications and proceed with caution, because your greatest danger is now in research and in the writing of the book. Once it's published it will not be in their [the Friends of Hekate's] interest to lay a finger on you because of the repercussions on them that a police investigation would entail. They can't touch you or those closely associated with you. They won't harm you physically—that would be to destroy their own ends.'

I had indeed wondered about the physical aspects, particularly in view of the deliberate hit and run 'accident' that had befallen Charles shortly after his secret meeting with the initiates of the Friends of Hekate. What would their reaction be when *The Demonic Connection* finally made the bookshops?

'But won't being upended from their favourite site in view of the book's disclosures, however carefully I may word them, provoke some sort of repercussion on their part?' I then asked Mary.

'They couldn't care less because they are so certain of themselves and sure that you will never discover anything, and even if you do, you wouldn't be able to use it or do anything about it. They won't stop you because they <u>are</u> so sure of themselves. Take Hitler. He was so sure of himself and so sure that nothing was going to stop him—and *he* was intercepting the powers of darkness. But it's not manual stuff now, it's mental,' she replied knowingly.

That last statement from Mary seemed to provide the key to the whole question concerning the Hekate group's future modus operandi. It would prove to be chillingly accurate in the years to come.

The Cell Fractures

I had deliberately withheld the information imparted by Mary from *The Demonic Connection*, intriguing though it was, because at the time much of it could not be verified. However, Andrew Collins and his team had been able to affirm some of Mary's material concerning the Friends of Hekate. The rest I had been able to confirm, mainly through researching books relating to the historical aspect—the relevance of which, in some cases, I had only recently come to realize, such was the depth of the subject material. But then, Mary had always emphasized that the Friends of Hekate were going into this very deeply, and it had become clear with the passing of each day that her comments were uncannily accurate in many instances.

I had been unable to introduce Andrew to Mary, because she had been suffering from an illness ever since 1986, and any attempt to test her on Bernard's psychic material at that time would have not only been grossly unfair to her, but may well have proved to be counterproductive generally. Alas, we would never be able to know the answer to that intriguing possibility, as Mary never recovered; sadly, in 1989, she died.

During that year, Andrew Collins began to broaden his base of information by working with other talented psychics. It was a policy that yielded results as far as the recovery of further important ritual artefacts was concerned. Acting on information received by one of his team, Andrew was able to unearth another ritual dagger from its burial place in the churchyard of Ide Hill church in Kent.

This was a locality that Andrew Collins was quite familiar with, as it had been used by the Black Alchemist in rites loosely based on the rituals of Zosimos of Panopolis, the fourth-century Greco-Egyptian alchemist. Ide Hill church, dedicated to St Mary the Virgin, is situated on top of a hill, a facet it has in common with Clapham.

Close to where the dagger had been exhumed, Andrew had also dug up a silver-plated chalice on which had been inscribed three symbols. The central symbol was the now familiar *Monas hieroglyphica*, left of this was the crab symbol, which was used as one of a series by Zosimos, and on the right was a serpent crawling out of the cup. It was the dagger, however, that produced the most interest.

The hilt of the dagger was shaped into the head of a griffin, with a protruding tongue. Also visible around the hilt was a tree trunk encircled by a snake, with a ball or egg in its mouth. The crosspiece of the dagger was shaped into a goat's skull on both sides, and along the blade were shown nude men and women reaching out towards animals. On one side was a goat and on the other a lamb, together with a cruder, smaller and more simplified engraving of a goat's skull. Around the griffin's neck was a piece of long, looped black cord, so the artefact was obviously worn

around somebody's neck, and this was confirmed when Andrew discovered a grey curly human hair, thought to be from a male's chest, attached to the griffin's head as if caught there while being worn.

The style of the goat dagger was very probably Jacobean, from around 1760, replicated by the Victorians (*c.* 1890), and while the quality of the brass was quite good the mouldings were a little cruder, which led us to believe that it may well have been a 20th-century copy of an earlier design. Its symbols, similar to the Hell Fire Club imagery of the 18th century, made it a perfect ritualistic dagger. The dagger was not used specifically for sacrifice (the blade was far too thick for that purpose) but as part of the important ritualistic activity that followed. Being so unique, it was shown to a number of occultists, none of whom had ever seen anything like it.

Andrew's team were of the opinion that this was the work of the former Friends of Hekate's centre (basically the same group reformed) along with other elite masters from the leading European orders. They were appropriating sanctified sites in order to create a power grid of interlinked areas and thus gain spiritual control of Britain's natural energy matrix.

Mary had spoken previously about the aims of the Friends of Hekate along virtually identical lines to Andrew's team. Nearly seven years later, they had been able to confirm her words—without any knowledge of what she had said. They also thought that the group had fragmented and that the process of using ancient sites in the manner that the Friends of Hekate were doing was part of their next stage of development.

An important period had been reached in the run-up to the turn of the millennium, as this was something that had been worked towards for a very long time.

As far as the goat dagger at the Ide Hill churchyard was concerned, Andrew's team felt that a festival called an 'octave' was relevant. This, of course, relates to the figure eight.

In the tarot ('the Book of Thoth') the number eight is the ogdoad, representing occult power, and number eight in the suit of Wands in the Minor Arcana is called 'eight magical wands'. In the Major Arcana, card number one—the magician—refers to the source of occult power and depicts the magician with a figure eight resting on its side immediately above his head. The exact point where the two circles join to form the figure '8' is in alignment with the ethereal 'third eye' (*ajna*) at the centre of the forehead, which is described by occultists as having ninety-six spokes, (twelve times eight) and is symbolic of seeing, when its potential is awakened, everything on the astral plane.

The eighth letter of the alphabet is 'h', but it is also linked with Venus and with 'opening' or 'womb'. Its occult number is the numerical equivalent of Venus, which is five, and according to author Fred Gettings in his *Encyclopedia of the Occult* (1980), it is also linked to the inverted pentagram. In addition, 'h' is often connected with 'e', the fifth letter of the alphabet, because of the similarity in the strength of sound of both letters; in occult theory this is more important than the spelling or natural order.

Apart from its obvious meaning, an octave is also a religious festival. It refers to a set of eight, starting with a festival and counting eight days from that to its octave. The eight-day time scale is important in this instance, as the goat dagger had apparently been planted in the earth some eight days before is was due to be retrieved by the group responsible in order for it to be 'charged up' with evil energies. The dagger was apparently planted after a ritual at midnight on Saturday, March 18, 1989, the day before the start of Passion Week—Palm Sunday. Good Friday, the day of Christ's crucifixion (in this instance the Good Friday falling on March 24, 1989) is considered to be the day when the Powers of Darkness are all-powerful, and it was on this day that Andrew had pulled the dagger from its charging place, thus interfering with and blocking a very important ritual. Like the demonic mural Charles had photographed at Clapham, the Ide Hill goat dagger was private to the group. It was something that was never meant to be seen, let alone seized by Andrew Collins. It was apparently due to be removed by the Group after another ritual at midnight on Easter Sunday, March 26—the day of Christ's rebirth and resurrection, the eighth day. This would have been when the reformed Hekate group, by their lore of reversal, would have been attempting to induce a birth of a very different nature—that is, the symbolic raising of the Antichrist.

Revelation and the Millennia

The coming of the Antichrist was first predicted, of course, in the awesome Book of Revelation, written by St John the Apostle, brother of James and son of Zebedee. Revelation issues a dire warning that there is a disembodied intelligence, which is malign, and remorselessly threatening to the existence of mankind. Generally speaking, the scriptures point towards a 'spiritual' rather than a physical mode of existence. The popular image of a horned, cloven-hoofed man with a tail is largely a Christian interpretation of the antediluvian figure of the coven

leader wearing an animal skin and horns of antlers. But it can also be derived from Man's associating intelligence with the human form. Lactantius refers to devils as '*spiritus tenues et incompréhensibles*' or 'thin, unseizable spirits'.

St John was banished to the Isle of Patmos where he received the vision of the Revelation *c.* AD 96. Once again the number seven turns up frequently in this book, with accounts of the seven vials, seven seals and seven visions, to name but three. In all there are fifty-four references to the number, including a seven-headed beast and dragon. The theme of various animals or beasts being seen as the 'devil's familiars' can be found everywhere in the Old Testament prophets. One passage is Isaias (XXXIV) which refers to dogs and wild cats, screech owls and crows and other creatures harder to identify, holding a demonic sabbath in the Land of Edom which, deserted and burnt down, has reverted to primeval chaos. Revelation uses the language of the Book of Enoch and some from the Old Testament, too, which is not dissimilar to the ancient Babylonian mythology.

At the opening of the first six seals there were 'revelations of the plan of judgement', but upon the opening of the seventh seal there followed a period of silence. The opening of this seal revealed the final 'things to come', which in their content were far more terrible than any of the foregoing ones, thus invoking a hushed silence.

In *The Mark of the Beast* (1990) co-authors Trevor Ravenscroft and Tim Wallace-Murphy search the symbolism of Revelation in the form of stone pillars at ancient sites. There were, apparently, seven sanctified sites, which had formerly marked the placements of the druids' seven planetary oracles. Seven cathedrals were later built on each of these sites. The alignment formed 'an apocalyptic constellation against the background of the zodiac'.

The druids believed that there were seven spirit-senses (organs of clairvoyance), which existed in the form of an earth alignment of Chakras embodied in the physical planet as well as in Man. Thus the druids created the sequenced oracles, all seven of which corresponded with the planets in our solar system—Moon, Mercury, Venus, Sun, Mars, Jupiter and Saturn. The locations they used can be found between Iberia and Scotland. The most significant oracle, the Sun, was placed in France on a site where later the Cathedral of Notre Dame de Chartres was built.

It was there that during the Middle Ages, an arcane Christian initiation centre—the Platonic School—formulated a clairvoyant calendar marked in stone, which predicts the crucial period of the Apocalypse as coming at the turn of the millennium. They were able to achieve this by creating a configuration using seven cathedrals, which were built on the seven planetary sites originally selected by the druids. The alignment occurs between the two Pillars of Wisdom and Strength at Rosslyn Chapel, at Roslin in Scotland, and Cintra, a small town not far from Lisbon in Portugal.

Tim Wallace-Murphy had suspected that an alignment of significantly sited and constructed cathedrals actually existed as part of a hidden configuration, 'built to represent the earth as the Temple of God as it is described in the Revelation'. He likens his search for the 'Apocalypse in stone' to that of the Grail, and ascertains the locations of the other oracles and their according cathedrals—Notre Dame de Paris marks the ancient placement of the Mars Oracle, for example, and Rosslyn Chapel, where a cathedral was once intended, stands on the site of the Saturn Oracle.

There is a legend connected to Rosslyn Chapel which concerns the murder carried out by a master mason (forerunners of the freemasons) of his apprentice. On returning from abroad the master mason had become so enraged at his apprentice for daring to design and complete a pillar in his absence, that he struck the unfortunate young man a killer blow to the right temple with his mallet.

In craft masonry, one of the initiation rituals involves the symbolic slaying of an apprentice—a blow to the right temple, administered by the master, for submitting a triangular stone rather than the obligatory square or rectangular stone. But when the lodge members discover that there is no stone fashioned to form the keystone of the royal arch they recover the apprentice's triangular one, which then assumes its correct place in the building. The apprentice ascends from his resting place and becomes the lodge's new Grand Master, his three-sided stone coming to represent the spiritual facets that are essential in order for man to develop spiritually.

The stone pillar that was designed and built by the apprentice at Rosslyn, according to the legend, was fittingly named the 'prentice pillar', and formed part of the alignment of the seven cathedrals. When this earthly alignment of planetary sites matches the alignment of planets in the sky, this is said to indicate the period in time when the critical point of the Apocalypse had been reached.

The sixth vision in Revelations ends with the release of Satan from confinement, his continued deception of the nations, the last rebellion against God, and the last universal war, the magnitude of which the world will have never seen before.

The seventh and last vision brings us to the turning point in time, at the end of the thousand-year reign of Christ upon Earth. However, in this

case the 'thousand' could relate to a denomination of 1000, so, in effect, it could be multiplied by two, bringing us to the year 2000.

The planetary alignment that comes closest to matching the earthly alignment of planetary sites at the seven cathedrals occurred in May 2000.

Perhaps for these reasons, many people, including occultists, have looked at the turn of the millennium as a period of spiritual awakening, a crucial point in time when the hieratical destiny of a country or continent can be shaped and subsequently controlled.

Chapter 6
Wheel of Misfortune

During the first two of my four interviews with Mary, the elderly Psychic, she had referred to 'the spokes of the Roman wheel' in connection with the history and activities of the Friends of Hekate. The phrase had both intrigued and perplexed me at the time. What was the significance of the 'Roman wheel', or 'the wheel' in connection with a dark magical hierarchy of this nature?

A wheel is, of course, a rotating circle, which in turn relates to the coiled serpent, its tail in the centre of hub. The image is identical with that of a Catherine wheel. The hub of the wheel was Winchester, the old English capital, and St Catherine's Hill is an important part of this area. The Romans were famous for their long straight roads connecting towns and villages like ley lines, which, as we know, connect ancient sites. But besides the metaphorical spokes that Mary had spoken of, did the term 'wheel' have some greater significance?

In the book *Magical and Mystical Sites in Europe and the British Isles* (1977) by Elizabeth Pepper and John Wilcock, Charles Walker discovered an ancient illustration associated with the dark side of the Moon Goddess, taken from a stone disc from Ionia, a province of what is now Turkey, in the sixth century BC. The drawing was called 'The Hekate Wheel' and its discovery had solved a riddle for Charles, who, some years earlier, in July 1983, had seen a cruder, less detailed engraving of the same symbol, measuring approximately eight inches in diameter, on a large stone at Sheeps Tor, Dartmoor. The book illustration (*see Figure 1*) seemed to sum up perfectly what we had ascertained about the Friends of Hekate.

The tiny centre, or hub, is encircled by six (the original number of the Beast) serpents rearing up and ready to smite anyone who attempts to penetrate to the centre. The serpents are all connected at the base to a perfect 'inner circle', thus providing supreme protection of the centre.

Outside the inner circle is a serpentine pattern of double lines circumventing it and so arranged as to suggest the continuous movements of writhing snakes, and thereby seeming to make entry to the Wheel of Hekate not only lengthy and circuitous for would-be initiates, but an absolute impossibility for unwanted outsiders.

In other words, this ancient stone mandala was perhaps the earliest illustration available of the 'malefic power spiral', and confirmed our earlier presumption that the Friends of Hekate had used or inaugurated this system of induction.

As our early ancestors were apparently aware of ley power or the natural energy force that flows between, and often converges at, sacred monuments and sanctified sites, it seems likely that what Mary referred to as 'the old condition of the Old Worship' was practised quite openly during the very early periods of pre-Christian history. If the first Hekate cult worship pervaded our shores during the 1000 BC period, did it then fuse with the 'Old Worship' that was already being openly practised? Was the Hekate Wheel then embodied into that infrastructure? If so, with the coming of the Celts, Romans and finally Christianity, Hekate's cult would have been forced underground, becoming a secret order, its doctrines available only to disciples, initiates and masters—its sanctity preserved. Is this what happened?

Origins of the Wheel

In witchcraft the 'Dance of the Wheel' is BC on Beltane, April 30/May 1. This major festival falls on one of the four cross-quarter days, and marks the second opening half of the turning wheel or year's cycle. The old Celtic year was divided into two halves, starting on Samhain (November 1, the beginning of winter, and Beltane, the start of summer). The old year's subdivisions then began on February 1 and August 1 respectively.

The interpretation of the May Eve Day festival in its archetypal form is

---

Fig 1 The Hekate Wheel, taken from a stone disc, Ionia, 6 BC.

Bel-, or Bel, or Balor. The origins of the name can be traced back to *baal*, which is Middle Eastern and means Lord. Some believe that Bel was the British counterpart of the old French-Celtic horned god Cernunnos, who was sometimes aspected with triple facets, like Hekate; Cernunnos, also like Hekate, was a leader of the Wild Hunt, which itself remains one of the most antiquated legends. But Cernunnos is seen as an underworld deity, or the 'dark one', whereas Bel was the 'bright one' associated with fire and light. In Britain, numerous statues of Cernunnos, or their remains, have been found at various sites, while on the site of the cathedral of Notre Dame in Paris, a temple once stood that was dedicated to Cernunnos.

In the 'old condition of worship' the Beltane ritual has a theme of sacrifice and rebirth, which climaxes with the sacrifice of a man representing the old Oak god. The hare and goat were also part of the sacrificial element of the ancient May fertility rites, though in later years the sacrificial aspect was made purely symbolic by substituting rushes or other plants or objects for humans and animals.

Samhain Eve—the Feast of the Dead, a partial return to primeval chaos more commonly known as Hallowe'en—takes place on October 31 and marks the commencement of the Celtic winter; on this day covens celebrate passing through the dark gates of the Lord of Death—one of the faces of Cernunnos.

Samhain Eve, too, has its own wheel symbolism. Part of one of the rituals involves the high priestess recounting a libation to Arianrhod, the goddess of the Silver Wheel. In *The Mysteries of Britain* (1925) Lewis Spence refers to an Arianrhod of the Silver Wheel as representing the constellation Corona Borealis, which is also associated with the fertility of the land.

Samhain Eve is the only festival other than the autumn equinox when the withershins (anti-clockwise) spiral dance is performed, creating a 'reverse energy movement'.

At the centre of the symbolic spiral is said to be Arianrhod, the Dark Goddess of death but also the bright goddess of rebirth and initiation; she is the triple goddess as well. Boreas, the mystical North Wind, is the gatekeeper of 'Caer Arianrhod', the Castle of the Silver Wheel. Robert Graves links Arianrhod with Ariadne, who is a goddess of sacrifice and rebirth. Her symbolism involves finding the centre of the labyrinth through the spiral thread. In old Celtic and Norse mythology, ageing kings were ritually burnt to death at Samhain because in the Old Worship this was seen as the main method of appeasing the gods and ensuring future fertility. But as with Beltane, this aspect applies only to the ancient Samhain festival; more modern interpretations involve adapting the rite to suit the purposes of the participants.

Candlemas (Imbolc) in February also uses wheel symbolism: whirling dancers carry blazing torches in a wheel formation, representing the return of the sun and the year's turning (see Chapter 2).

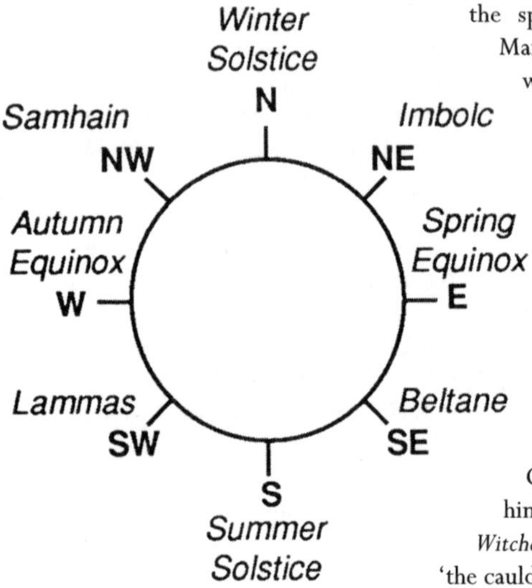

The *Book of Shadows* appropriated by Gerald Baron Gardner states that for the spring equinox festival on March 21 'the symbol of the wheel should be placed on the altar, flanked with burning candles, or fire in some form'. Janet and Stewart Farrar in their informative book *Eight Sabbats for Witches* (1981) suggest that 'the solar fire-wheel is a genuine equinoctial tradition, and not merely a gap-filling choice of Gardner's', while Gardner himself, writing in his book *Witchcraft Today* (1954), refers to 'the cauldron of regeneration and the dance of the wheel', stating that it was usually performed on or near December 22. In fact the belief that a witch or similar occultist could transform themselves into a wheel was once quite widespread. But if Lewis Spence's theories are correct then the origins of these ancient rites stem from North Africa and were appropriated from resident British Iberians by the Celts (see Chapter 2).

The way in which the wheel and its symbolic imagery are incorporated into festival rites varies from group to group and from sabbat to sabbat.

The eight festivals or witches' sabbats directly relate to the eight directions of what is known as the sacred British wheel. In *The Ancient British Goddess* (1991) by Kathy Jones there is an illustration that shows the dates of the eight sabbats (the solstices, equinoxes and cross-quarter days)

Fig 2 The ancient British wheel. Was the wheel symbolism appropriated by a secret Templar order, which also took its title from the same? If so, is that organization still in existence today?

and how they correspond with the compass points. At the top is the winter solstice, December 21, which is at the northern point of the compass. Then Candlemas, at the beginning of February, is at the north-east, and so on right round to Samhain on November 1, which lies at the north-west.

Now I could see how this imagery might relate to various points on the natural landscape where ancient sites of apparent magical potency were—if indeed the sites could be aligned in some sort of circular grouping, as Mary had previously indicated.

A member of Andrew Collins's new psychic team, Fiona, had suggested that the Friends of Hekate were commandeering the 'calendar of the witches' in their rituals. She had referred to only six festivals instead of the customary eight—but bearing in mind the Hekate Wheel's symbolism of the six snakes possibly relating to six celebrations as part of the yearly cycle, this would make perfect sense.

The symbolism of a rotating wheel containing furls of serpents also signifies movement, fluidity and change. The activities of Hekate's cult at pagan and other sanctified sites down the ages had not necessarily been constant. Mary had felt as much when she had said that 'this type of worship will always break out from time to time.'

Like Hekate, Diana had her own wheel symbolism, which relates to the spinning wheel. Doreen Valiente refers to this as a 'very ancient myth— the myth of Fate, the spinner, the great goddess who spins human life. She spun the lives of all men: all things were spun from the wheel of Diana'.

Were there any other examples of wheel symbolism to be found in connection with this or any other cult?

St Catherine's Cult

While writing up the material for his latest occult book, *The Second Coming* (1993), Andrew Collins phoned me about an intriguing discovery he had made. A historical source had

Fig 3 St Catherine's Wheel.

referred to Winchester's Chapel of St Catherine, situated on St Catherine's Hill, as being founded by Henry de Blois, Bishop of Winchester at the time when the 'cult of St Catherine was at its height'. The statement led the reader to assume that Henry de Blois was influenced by or involved with this cult in some manner.

A member of Andrew's psychic team, Helen, had used the term 'Dark Council' in relation to the reformed Friends of Hekate. It was Helen who had provided the vital clues and information that had led to Andrew recovering the goat dagger at Ide Hill and thus preventing an important ritual that Helen had psychically visualized; he knew her material to be accurate.

However, second impressions revealed that the 'Dark Council' had apparently been an influential body of medieval high churchmen allegedly practising a form of heresy in Winchester, which involved the mysteries of St Catherine's cult. Helen had previously picked up the name 'Dark Council' in relation to St Catherine's Hill, and immediately applied it to the present day.

Andrew was sure that Henry de Blois figured prominently in this Dark Council, and that this particular lineage of gnostic adulation stretched down to the mid-14th century and the time of Edward III, the Black Prince. Because Andrew's deadline for delivering the finished manuscript of *The Second Coming* was looming, he wasn't in a position to carry out as much research on these matters as he would have liked, which placed the ball firmly in my court.

St Catherine of Alexandria was royal, rich and learned. After she repelled the advances of Emperor Maximian (or Maximinus—there are varying accounts in different books) the emperor first had her imprisoned then tied and bound to a spiked wheel. This appears to have been an early version of a complex instrument of torture. It comprised four wheels armed with knives and teeth that were turned in different directions.

According to some versions, Catherine miraculously survived this and other attempts to break her before her enraged captor finally ordered her to be beheaded in AD 307. Her body was discovered *c.* AD 800 at Mount Sinai, where a Templar-style order, the Knights of St Catherine, was later inaugurated in 1063.

She became a patron saint of the Knights Templar after being adopted by the medieval crusaders in 1099. The name Catherine is derived from the Greek *cathar*, meaning pure, which has probably earned her adulation among gnostics.

Some kind of oil or similar substance apparently oozed from St

Catherine's bones for many years after her death. The monks on Mount Sinai collected this fluid, and the saint's fame began to spread throughout Europe. In 1330 Henry II of Brunswick visited her remains and was said to have removed a small bone and brought it back to Europe. In 1229 King Louis IX of France had a church dedicated to St Catherine built in Paris.

Gnosticism originated in Egypt, and many magical incantations and other elements from Egyptian magic and underworld worship were incorporated into this new doctrine. It was a mixture that also included Indian, Babylonian and Christian creeds, though the Church and orthodox Christians viewed it with the utmost contempt. Several wide-ranging sects were able to exist and thrive under the gnostics' umbrella.

The majority of sects contained a secular priesthood of initiates, practising various magical arts and discovering the mysteries. The term 'gnostic' is derived from the Greek meaning 'to know'. The gnostics believed that the path to our true destiny lay in passing through the planetary spheres, a passage defended by a planetary spirit guardian, or Archon. The Archons were the arch enemies of the gnostics, and their impenetrable barrier to the godhead could only be breached by knowing key words, phrases and threats which only Gnosticism could provide.

The gnostics believed that the universal creator was not the supreme god to whom all Christians and much of the rest of mankind gave credence for their existence on this planet, but was instead a bogus, mediocre deity whose domination must be defied through non-procreation. To subject future generations to an earthly existence would be to condemn them to an alien way of life, many gnostics believed. They reversed the old biblical teachings, in some cases saying that the Devil was in fact a good angel—an enemy of Jehovah whom they identified as siding with the Archons.

It was a strange sect, often embracing diverse viewpoints. For example, some denounced Christ as the son of the evil Jehovah and instead honoured Judas Iscariot's treachery for his hand in the crucifixion. Most believed that Jesus was a holy saviour who had come to earth to release mankind from this 'God of the Jews'. This section of gnostics, while acknowledging Jesus Christ, nonetheless believed that God was an evil consort of the Archons; their practices were considered to be heretical. In general the gnostics thought that the way to break the stranglehold being applied to mankind by the evil Jehovah and the Archons was to flout all the commandments; some of them might argue in favour of the 'deadly sins'. Indeed several concluded that good and evil were only human sentiments that meant nothing, given that their path to achieving total spiritual enlightenment was to experience everything; this route would take them

close to some fundamental magical beliefs but would nonetheless be at odds with their roots in Zoroastrian dualism.

Summing up the gnostics in *The Black Arts* (1969) Richard Cavendish says:

> 'All these gnostic ideas fit into the general pattern of Satanism; indeed, they largely established it. There is no evidence that any of the gnostics consciously worshipped the Devil, but it is not surprising that orthodox Christians thought they did. After the triumph of Christianity and its adoption as the state religion of the Roman Empire, gnostic theories were kept alive by obscure heretical sects in the East and were eventually transmitted into Western Europe.'

In *The Cult of the Black Virgin* (1985) Ean Begg identifies St Catherine with a forbidden gnostic Christian cult that was forced underground after the 'Victory of the Cross' only to re-emerge centuries later during the time of the Crusades. There's a strong suggestion that this adoration resurfaced with Cathar worship in southern France. St Catherine is also linked with the Black Virgin cult, where at Mount Sinai a Black Virgin was reputedly dedicated to her.

In *The Second Coming* Andrew Collins concludes that St Catherine also incorporates the darker aspects of Dark Goddesses like Hekate; the two are, of course, linked through the use of wheel symbolism. St Catherine also relates to the midnight sun or full-Moon eclipse, which is seen as an important time of magical efficacy in adept circles. Her feast day falls on November 25, which commemorates the Wheel Goddess of the Underworld. Here Catherine is twinned with Arianrhod, Persephone Kore and Proserpina, and is described in old pagan law as Queen of the Shades, ruler of the souls of the dead—titles that are also bestowed on Hekate.

Like Arianrhod's, St Catherine's Wheel is silver, containing six spokes as shown in her emblem. In trying to prohibit paganism, the Church had converted pagan gods into saints but had found the task of expurgating paganism and goddess worship virtually impossible in some parts of Europe and the Middle East.

St Mercury also shares his feast day with St Catherine. In the book *The Witches' Goddess* (1987) by Janet and Stewart Farrar, Charles found an interesting link with Oshun and Oyo, goddesses of the Nigerian Yoruba tribe. They were sisters, and were taken to Brazil by slaves, where they became voodoo goddesses, identified with St Barbara and St Catherine.

Oshun (spelt Oxun in Brazil) is patroness of the zodiacal sign Capricorn.

The Voodoo Damballah

The cult of voodoo began in Africa and was taken to Brazil and the Caribbean, the image of the Damballah is at the heart of voodoo magic. Damballah is the serpent god and the voodoo serpent, which devours its own tail. Damballah fortifies this link, with the universal theme of the circle being depicted as 'the self turned inwards upon itself'.

The symbol of the Damballah is of particular interest to us. This image is in the form of a wheel constructed from three circles or grades and containing twelve straight spokes or spikes. For the initiate it stands for the 'geometric perfection of the mysteries'.

To begin with there are obvious similarities with the Hekate Wheel. The Damballah also contains a tiny centre and this is formed by an ouroboros serpent, devouring its own tail. The second ring or circle is constructed in an identical manner to the centre. Eleven out of the twelve spokes extend beyond the outer ring as they spread outwards from the small centre. On top of each of the eleven extending spokes is the head of a serpent facing outwards as if to signify full protection from any intruders. The twelfth spoke forms the apex, at the head of which is the design of a magic square containing what appear to be the phases of the Moon.

In the past occult writers have drawn attention to certain similarities between Egyptian and voodoo magical symbolism. For example, at the centre of the voodoo temple is the sign of the rising sun, represented by an upright wooden post or comparable vertical, surrounded by various symbols. This

Fig 4 The voodoo 'Damballah'.

is similar to the sun on the horizon in Egypt, which also contains the same symbols.

The cult of St Catherine is linked to the period of the midnight sun and thereafter until sunrise. The Damballah incorporates much of the symbolism that is contained in the image of the 'spiked' wheel to which St Catherine of Alexandria was tied. In fact the spokes of the Damballah could also be interpreted as spikes, as they extend beyond the wheel's circumference and are 'spiked' with serpent heads pointing outwards.

The association of a voodoo goddess with St Catherine, together with the symbolic linking of the Damballah with both the Catherine and Hekate Wheels, leads us to ask whether aspects of St Catherine's cult and Hekate's cult were embodied at some stage in the mysteries of voodoo. And what exactly was Bishop Henry de Blois's involvement with the cult of St Catherine during medieval times in Britain?

Chapter 7
Talismans of Torment

As Bishop of Winchester and brother of King Stephen, Henry de Blois had been able to amass considerable wealth, which had in part been used to finance the construction of various religious buildings. This had helped endear the bishop to the medieval ecclesiastical hierarchy. However, various references in books had alerted Andrew Collins to the strong probability that Henry de Blois's religious convictions and indulgences had exceeded the bounds of his monastic oaths. St Bernard of Clairvaux, for example, had referred to him as 'a rival pope—the old wizard and whore of Winchester'.

From 1126 until his death in 1171, Henry de Blois was Abbot of Glastonbury, where peculiar Christian gnostic religious practices had apparently regularly taken place. A 14th-century seal from Glastonbury Abbey depicts St Catherine in a prominent place alongside the Virgin Mary.

When the coffin of Henry's predecessor at Glastonbury, Abbot Seffrid Pelochin, was opened in Chichester hundreds of years later, an episcopal ring made from jasper and containing an effigy of the gnostic serpent god Abraxas was found still attached to one of the fingers on his skeletal hand.

Abraxas is a mystical name of likely gnostic origin. The Abraxas image is one of a cock-headed man bearing a whip and shield and with the legs and feet of a serpent. This form became associated with the demonic god, the image being carved onto gems or stones.

The Abraxas ring originated with the movement of the Christian gnostic eccentric Basilides, who taught at Alexandria between the years AD 120 and 140, just 150 years before the time of St Catherine herself at the same city.

Basilides of Alexandria was the most celebrated of gnostics, according to author Kurt Seligman (*Magic, Supernaturalism and Religion*, 1971). Basilides claimed to have received his abstruse teachings directly from Glaucus, who had been a disciple of the apostle Peter.

The Basilides system comprised three grades—material, intellectual and spiritual. It operated in a similar manner to sects involved in Jewish cabbalism and was also said to possess doctrines that were akin to those of the Ophites. The cult of the Ophites had embraced Egyptian occult rites along with serpent symbolism, which became the focus of their mysteries. Several sects of the Ophites worshipped the ouroboros serpent, which is coiled in a circle and seen to be biting its own tail, and represents a continuous cycle containing both good and evil.

Alexandria, the Ancient Egyptian city, was the hub of gnostic worship. The gnostics there held in high esteem the anthology of fragmented rituals known as 'The Chaldean Oracles', which first appeared in the second century AD (see Chapter 2). A central belief of these teachings was that Hekate was the Great Mother or the universal life force itself.

The gnostics had endeavoured to bring about a fusion of pagan rituals and Christianity, which resulted in a composite form of heresy. The majority of them spurned the symbol of the cross, seeing it as a symbol of satanic evil, an instrument by which and on which Jesus was murdered by the emissaries of the Satan–Jehovah conspiracy.

For their own beliefs, the Basilides sect vehemently adhered to Abraxas, which remained at the heart of their doctrines. Abraxas relates to the number 365 for the god who ruled each year and each of its 'attributes' or days. The letters of the Greek alphabet also corresponded to numbers—the letters of Abraxas add up to 365. The solar cycle symbolism of Abraxas also links to the wheel, its full revolution representing the yearly cycle; the followers of Basilides may well have conceived the name Abraxas for that purpose.

They also believed that the name Abraxas contained great mysteries, as it was composed of the seven Greek letters that go to make up the number 365. Abraxas was seen by the Basilidian sect as their supreme god who had sent Christ to earth in the form of a mere phantom. It is certain that this adulation was practised at the time of St Catherine of Alexandria and continued for centuries afterwards.

It seems likely, too, that Henry de Blois introduced the Glastonbury monks to the mysteries of St Catherine's cult. At the same time Henry was able to weald considerable power and influence upon his elder brother King Stephen.

Henry I, the old king, had died on December 1, 1135 and his daughter and natural heir, Matilda, had expected to be crowned queen. However, it was her cousin Stephen de Blois who moved fleetingly and ruthlessly to gain the throne at Westminster on December 22, 1135, thus usurping Matilda.

In his book *The Devil's Crown* (1978) Richard Barber strongly implies that Henry de Blois was the 'instigator of the plot to install his elder brother as king'. He was also instrumental in prevailing upon the treasurer, William de Font de l'Arche, to hand over the treasury together with Winchester Castle. The Oxford 'History of England' series *Domesday Book to Magna Carta, 1087–1216* by A. L. Poole, refers to the period of Stephen's reign simply as 'the anarchy, 1135–1154'.

In *A Short History of the English People* (1889) historian John Richard Green says of King Stephen's rule: 'The nineteen years of his reign are years of a misrule and disorder unknown in our history'. Green also says of Henry de Blois: 'Henry of Winchester, however, half monk, half soldier, as he was called, possessed too little religious influence to wield a really spiritual power; it was only at the close of Stephen's reign that the nation really found a moral leader in Theobald, the Archbishop of Canterbury.' That statement provides us with the clearest indication yet that despite Henry de Blois's vast material wealth and personal influence over his brother and the realm, spiritually and in his religious practices he had moved right away from being able to exercise any influence over ordinary people and the nation as a whole, though he still held away with the monastic grandees. In other words, what Green is really implying is that Henry de Blois was spiritually and morally unfit to hold such office in the Church.

There were other indications, too, of how the Church's spiritual influence had deteriorated alarmingly under his stewardship. In 1143 he held a meeting of the synod in London, which his brother King Stephen also attended. This was on account of the fact that the clergy had been so reduced in numbers that bandits, chancing their luck, were taking some clergymen hostage and holding them to ransom in the hope that their desperate superiors would pay up. The synod therefore decreed that anyone who 'laid violent hands on a cleric' would be punished, but the decree had little effect in practice.

Ten years later, Archbishop Theobald was attempting to repair some of the damage that had been done during Stephen's rein by forming a peace agreement. He was helped by Henry de Blois, who had repented and tried to put an end to the 'evils' he had been instrumental in creating. Henry had played a crucial political role throughout his brother Stephen's reign. He had even upstaged this patron of the arts by decorating his own episcopal palace with antique sculptures purchased in Rome.

The inscriptions on two gilded and enamelled self-commemorative

plaques, which were attached to a small movable altar, provide us with clues as to Henry's opinion of himself. The plaques depict him presenting his altar to heaven, and one of the inscriptions reads as follows: 'Art comes before gold and gems, the author before everything. Henry, alive in bronze, gives gifts to God. Henry, whose fame commends him to men, whose character commends him to the heavens, a man equal in mind to the Muses, and in eloquence higher than Marcus.' The bishop's exulted opinion of himself was certainly more on a par with some sort of self-styled magus heading a gnostic secret cult than humbler Christian cleric.

The legend of the muses involves traditions in Greek mythology. Hesiod's generally accepted account was that the muses were the nine daughters of Zeus and the Titanes Mnemosyne. Their cult started in Thrace. They have been associated by occultists with the music of the spheres or planetary ratios. A more modern interpretation of the older occult theory is that this music can only be heard by initiates whilst they exist in the physical plane but that it becomes part of the afterlife experience for everyone else.

In Greek mythology the Muses were closely linked to the Apollo cult. They were the patrons of poetry and guardians of the Delphi Oracle, where they were venerated along with Apollo. However, as goddesses the muses were quickly upset and pitilessly punished those who had the temerity to vie with them.

For Henry de Blois to set himself up as a 'man equal in mind' to such occult legends was yet another indication as to his probable gnostic leanings. Marcus, referred to at the end of the inscription, was quite probably the historical figure of Marcus Aurelius Antoninus, the second-century Roman Emperor. He persecuted the Christians for political gains but became well-known for his meditations of a philosophical nature. He was generally regarded as one of the best Roman emperors—another rather bizarre figure for Bishop Henry to compare himself with, assuming I am correct.

The cover of a psalter specially made for Bishop Henry shows a huge satanic reptilian head sprouting horns decorated with dragon's ears. Inside the satanic figurehead's enormous gaping mouth are a number of arch-demons and other figures, including a crowned king and queen, plus one other crowned body. Two of the crowned bodies can be clearly seen hanging upside down, including the bearded king, who has a noose around his neck. Such a portrayal of royalty could be interpreted as a sign of political adroitness on behalf of Henry de Blois. The whole painting is framed within a patterned border but outside is an angel looking rather mournful and turning a key to the door of damnation, thus ensuring that everyone inside of Satan's mouth is kept soundly locked in.

Henry's cousin Matilda, daughter of Henry I and the rightful successor to the throne, had married Geoffrey Plantagenet, son of Fulk Comte d'Anjou. The name 'Plantagenet' derives from the sprig of broom, *planta genista*, worn in the helmets of the fearless dukes of Anjou in battle, and adopted by Geoffrey, the Angevin who fathered Henry II.

In her book *An ABC of Witchcraft Past and Present* (*op. cit.*) Doreen Valiente links the Plantagenet dynasty through its dark Angevin history with the very roots of European witchcraft. The Angevin dynasty was said to have been born from a long line of pagans, but the implication here is that they practised a debased form of the Old Religion and that the Plantagenet badge adopted by Geoffrey was a cult sigil or talisman.

The most notorious of the Angevins, according to J. R. Green, was Fulk the Black, who was 'the first in whom we can trace that marked type of character which their House was to preserve with a fatal constancy through two hundred years'. That type of character was all too evident when, devoid of any natural affection, Fulk the Black had his wife burnt at the stake: it is said of him that 'in Fulk there first appeared the low type of superstition which startled even superstitious ages in the early Plantagenets.'

The Wild Hunt

There is also a Wild Hunt legend that connects the Angevin dynasty to Hekate. This was a host, or rout, of followers known as the Wild Hunt, which was led usually by Hekate or her appropriate localized form, bearing torches that gave a mysterious, unearthly light, and accompanied by the inevitable hounds.

This ghostly procession would roam the countryside by night in an orgy of destruction, but instead of the silence usually associated with apparitions, a cacophony of terrifying sound always accompanied the Wild Hunt. The sounds were of snakes hissing as they entwined themselves in the goddess's hair, and of the infernal long-toothed hounds howling and snarling at her feet.

The hunt's followers comprised all manner of apparitions, part human, part animal, child-eaters, blood-suckers, ready to indulge themselves in whatever form of malevolent magic their leader would require of them under cover of darkness. These were akin to the wild men and women, the hunters and huntresses who link up with Diana and Hekate. In *A History of Witchcraft, Sorcerers, Heretics and Pagans* (1980), Jeffrey B. Russell tells us that

'Diana was identified with three-faced Hekate, dread pale goddess of death, patroness of evil sorcery, and mother of Lamias. In this dark form, Diana appeared in early medieval belief as a leader of witch processions and rites. But the origins of these Dianic processions, unknown in Rome, are more Teutonic than Mediterranean and have their roots in the Wild Hunt.'

However, one ritual that became associated with the Wild Hunt does stem from the Mediterranean—the winter solstice ritual known as the Lenaea or Festival of the Wild Women, performed in Athens. This was originally a sacrifice and rebirth ritual involving the harvest-god Dionysos, whereby the human counterpart was ripped apart and devoured by the nine wild women. But as with most rites it became adapted in later times with the human victim being replaced by a goat kid. The wild women are also part of the Norse version of the Wild Hunt, where they are known as the Valkyries—terrible warrior women who decided who was to be their next victim by reading omens in blood left by their previous one, or similar. They rode with Woden or Odin in the northern tradition—probably one of the most time-worn versions of the Wild Hunt.

The leaders of the Wild Hunt have a tendency to vary in identity from region to region—and also in gender. The leader was sometimes male. Herne, the hunter, is said to lead the Wild Hunt around Windsor Great Park in England. Herne is the central figure in many legends, whose origins, according to author Eric Maple, 'are so very ancient that [they] are now untraceable' (*Supernatural England*, 1977). Herne was often associated with the Devil because his name relates to 'brightness' and the cult of the Moon, as does Hekate's.

In Stephen Ronan's book *The Goddess Hekate* (1992), a section by K. F. Smith refers to a French leader of the Wild Hunt. In Touraine, the figure of Foulques Nerra, the ancestor of the Plantagenets, 'still roams through the darkness with his immaterial host'—a clear indication that Hekate and her crew 'are only disguised, not outworn'. Foulques Nerra was, in actuality, none other than Fulk the Black himself.

The French Connection

The monstrous crimes of Fulk the Black were abominable even by medieval standards. Using accounts taken from the *Chroniques d'Anjou*, published by the Historical Society of France (Paris, 1856–71), J. R. Green sums up the rule of Fulk the Black as follows: 'Familiar as the age was with treason and rapine and blood, it recoiled from the cool cynicism of his crimes, and believed the wrath of Heaven to have been revealed against the union of the worst forms of evil in Fulk the Black.'

His mother was reputedly a mysterious demon princess called Melusine whom his father, Geoffrey Grey-Gown, had married for her beauty; it was not known where she had come from. She rarely attended Mass, appearing apprehensive on the rare occasions that she did go, and always leaving before the main part of the Mass. Count Geoffrey was insistent on discovering why, so he ordered four men to hold her back the next time she tried to leave. When they grabbed her cloak, she simply slid out of it and disappeared through a window with a scream, never to be seen again. It was said that Fulk's mother had brought 'demon blood' into the House of Anjou. Indeed, Fulk the Black's barbarous fifty-year reign, which ended with his death in 1040, had terrified everyone, including the French king, and had made Anjou the greatest province in France.

The story of Melusine is made even more mysterious by varying accounts of exactly when she entered the Angevin dynasty. Some versions put her marriage at an earlier period and have her bearing two sons, from whom the later counts were descended. There were said to have been 'many strange things about Melusine'. Even Fulk Nerra's successor, Count Fulk Rechin, admitted that he had no knowledge of his first three ancestors. The first generally accepted Count of Anjou was Fulk the Good (941 to 960). His son, Geoffrey Grey-Gown, followed him (*c.* 960 to 987), to be succeeded in turn by Fulk Nerra/Fulk the Black in 987.

During his fearful rule Fulk the Black had also robbed the Church of land and had been generally contemptuous of its ecclesiastical doctrines. But fearing the arrival of his own judgement day, in an extraordinary religious U-turn, Fulk undertook no fewer than three pilgrimages to Jerusalem. This was an amazing feat, considering that few people made the journey even once in those days.

Towards the end of his first journey to Jerusalem Fulk Nerra was led under escort to the city gates where at first he was refused entry. Once he had paid for himself and the other poorer pilgrims, he was allowed in, but access to the Lord's Tomb was denied him and would only be granted if he performed a strange ritual there. Rather unwillingly he agreed. Fulk acquired the bladder of a ram, which he freed from decontaminants before filling it with the best wine. He placed this peculiar apparatus between his thighs, and after removing his shoes, approached the Lord's tomb and poured the wine from the ram's bladder over it. The guards, perhaps realizing that he was a corrupt pagan, had tried to trick him into urinating on the tomb. Fulk and his entire entourage were admitted to the tomb where, after shedding numerous tears of repentance, Fulk claimed to have felt a form of divine power when the tomb's hard stone softened to his touch. He left the site in a fury as some in his party had poured scorn over his new religious experience, but by giving generously to the needy Fulk had the last laugh: the Syrians gave him a piece of the holy cross that was guarding the tomb. The cunning of Fulk Nerra had once again turned a potentially difficult situation to his advantage.

Fulk had two children by his wife: a son, Geoffrey Martel, and a daughter, Adela. On Fulk's death in 1040, his son Geoffrey Martel took over the House of Anjou, but because Geoffrey had no sons himself, the line of succession passed to his nephews, Geoffrey the Bearded and Fulk Rechin, with the lands of Anjou and the conquered Touraine being divided between them. Such were the deeds carried out by and on behalf of these two men that one account in the *Plantagenet Chronicles* refers to 'the number and nature of evils which occurred in the county' while they were in power. In fact the chronicler feels torn: 'their disclosure is ordered by true history but forbidden by the horror and scale of the destruction.'

In 1066 Fulk Rechin captured and imprisoned his brother before assuming control of the region. He made a pact with Stephen, Count of Blois, which helped Fulk secure his position as Count of Anjou by keeping his helpless brother bound in chains.

Once again the dark Angevin past had come to manifest itself, this time in the form of Fulk Rechin, whose evil exploits may never be fully accounted for. He caused the French barons to go to war with each other and created a climate of treachery and turmoil that made the House of Anjou vulnerable to its enemies. Although William the Conqueror had temporarily halted the advance of the House of Anjou—and it was allowed to slide further by the inept administration of Count Fulk Rechin—it nonetheless rose with fresh vigour when his son in turn, Fulk V of Jerusalem, succeeded him. This new Count of Anjou was the one enemy that Henry I of England feared above all others.

In order to disarm his restless hostility, Henry I gave to Fulk's son, Geoffrey Plantagenet, the hand in marriage of his widowed daughter Matilda—the rightful heir to the English throne. This arranged marriage took place in 1128. Matilda was twenty-five years old while Geoffrey, the heir to Anjou and Maine, was just fourteen. This disastrous union, shrouded in secrecy from the beginning, brought nothing but strife and civil war to this country, heralding the decades of misrule and disorder that followed this questionable French connection.

Matilda detested her juvenile husband, whom she felt was completely beneath her in social standing. For his part, Geoffrey felt equal antipathy towards her, yet both parties possessed enough political cunning to make the fullest use of their cold-hearted bond. Matilda was rigid, contemptuous and unfeminine while Geoffrey, in spite of his good looks (he was known as Geoffrey the Handsome) was also callous and implacable. Some might well say that they were, in theory, well suited.

Their son, Henry of Anjou, succeeded Stephen to the throne in 1154, aged twenty-one, and became Henry II, the first of the Plantagenet kings and one of the most powerful monarchs in Western Europe. He added Aquitaine and Gascony to the Angevin Empire, becoming King of England, Duke of Normandy and Aquitaine while also being the Count of Anjou. He displayed certain Angevin characteristics, which made many afraid of him.

Ralph Niger, a cleric, rebuked Henry for not attending church enough and for appearing ill at ease on the occasions when he did choose to be present, often mumbling to himself during Mass and appearing to be disengaged in some manner from the surroundings. Henry was a charismatic ruler, giving generously to the poor and needy and founding several houses of religion, but he was also venomous and unforgiving towards anyone who had the temerity to upset him.

He will be remembered chiefly for ordering the murder of Becket, Archbishop of Canterbury, in 1170, an act that caused him to be utterly disgraced in the eyes of the dying Bishop of Winchester, Henry de Blois.

As with his own brother Stephen, Henry de Blois had done much to help the young Angevin succeed to the throne some sixteen years earlier. Whatever his faults might have been, the ailing bishop could not possibly have condoned Becket's murder. What's more, Henry de Blois was intimately aware of the facts surrounding the dispute between the king and the archbishop, and pointed the finger of blame directly at Henry II during a disturbing death-bed visitation by the monarch. This, apparently, made such a deep impression on Henry II that he had to spend a month in Wales in order to gather himself together (and improve relations with the Welsh princes).

Henry's two sons were Richard I and John, in whom the Angevin characteristic of unbridled cruelty was all too apparent. Both had violent tempers, and by their monstrous behaviour caused St Bernard, Cistercian Abbot of Clairvaux in France, to say of them: 'From the Devil they came and to the Devil they shall return'.

The Houses of Anjou and Blois had not only controlled much of France, but they had also elevated themselves to the very pinnacle of British rule with the enthronement of kings Stephen and Henry respectively and the continuation of the Anjou line upon the throne. The aura of demonic attributes and mysteries that surrounded the House of Anjou marked its

incumbents as more than mere mortals, which doubtless contributed to their hold on power in both England and France for many generations.

Fulk V of Jerusalem, father of Geoffrey Plantagenet and grandfather to Henry II, while being an awesome opponent in the Angevin tradition, was nonetheless generally considered to be more upright and charitable in attitude towards the men of God than any of his predecessors had been. Yet there was no escaping his ancestry, and the mystique surrounding the House of Anjou and whole Plantagenet line was further added to by the fact that Fulk V, son of the evil Fulk Rechin, was one of the early Knights Templar.

The Altar of the Templars

The Knights Templar were formed in 1118. Known also as the Poor Knights of the Temple of Solomon, they were said to be only nine in number. However, records show that by 1128 there were some additional members: Hugues de Champagne, and Fulk V Comte d'Anjou.

Their origins are believed to lie in the secret societies of the Sufis and the Assassins of ancient Persia. Through Zoroastrianism and Middle Eastern dualism, the Assassins and Sufis were also linked to the gnostics and the Cathars as well as several other sects of mystery.

The Assassins were led by Hasam and based in a Persian castle some 600 feet above a valley pass. After the death of Hasam in 1124, the Assassins continued to exist in much the same manner as their name suggests—they were paid by the European crusaders to eliminate foes of the crusaders; they were, in effect, the original contract killers. The order was forced to fragment, however, in 1256 after being ousted by the Mongols. The Assassins were apparently instrumental in instructing the Hindu death cult known as the thugs or thuggee, who were devotees of the goddess Kali, also known as Kali 'the Black'—the destroyer, who is in turn both wife and mother to Shiva, the god of destruction and rebirth.

The thuggees, or phansigars (noose users), strangled unsuspecting travellers from behind with speed and deadly precision using a knotted scarf known as a rumal. Their organization was elaborate and meticulous. They would operate in gangs, using scouts to locate their intended victims before two phansigars carried out the ritual murder whilst one extra thug held the victim down. They regarded this type of ceremonial assassination as a divine duty dedicated to Kali.

The Kali cult lasted until the early 19th century and was responsible for thousands of sacrificial killings before being eventually suppressed by the British Raj.

The most sacred emblem of the Kali devotees was the pickaxe in the shape of a sickle or scythe, which was consecrated in a detailed ritual, being passed through fire seven times by the thugs. The name 'Assassins' cropped up during a 19th-century court case in Bombay, when a Persian Prince laid claim to lineage from the original Grand Master of the order.

The Assassins and the Sufis are said to be linked with ancient goddess worship through their utilization of the double axe emblem, not dissimilar to the Kali worshippers' pickaxe, and the traits of rituals they carried out. Some of the artefacts that were discovered among the remains of the Assassins' mountain fortress had a pentagram inscribed upon them. The exact origins of the Assassins remain unknown, as their library at Alamut, which contained books of their rituals, was burnt down in 1256; they are thought, though, to have been tentatively associated with Gnosticism. The Sufis' inception was believed to have occurred some 40,000 years ago in Central Asia. If this theory—offered by J. G. Bennett in his book *The Masters of Wisdom* (1977)—is true, then Sufism must be considered one of the oldest cults in the Old Worship syndrome.

In *The Occult Conspiracy* (1989) Michael Howard links together these occult and ancient religious orders. Of the Assassins he says: 'They also wore white tunics and a red sash, symbolizing innocence and blood, which is similar to the costume adopted by the Zoroastrians, the Sufis, the Cathars and the Templars.' Writing in the book *Secret Societies*, David Annan takes the link between the Assassins and Templars further by saying: 'There is little question that Hugues de Payens, the Burgundian knight who founded the Order of the Temple in 1118 with eight other knights and 'poor fellow-soldiers of Christ' modelled his organization on that of the Assassins. The two organizations certainly knew each other in Syria before 1128, when the Templar Rule was written. The division of the Templars under their Grand Master, into grand priors, priors, knights, esquires and lay brothers closely follows the traditional hierarchy of the Assassins.'

The year of 1128 was also a good one for the House of Anjou largely due to the ingenious administration of Fulk V of Jerusalem. Fulk had acquired the title 'King of Jerusalem' which had been bestowed upon him with the help of Louis VIII of France. King Baldwin II of Jerusalem had no heirs, so he had asked Louis to select an appropriate French nobleman to marry his eldest daughter Melisande and thereby assume the Crown of Jerusalem once the old king had died.

In 1129 Fulk journeyed to the Middle East once more—this time to marry Melisande, and he became King of Jerusalem shortly afterwards on King Baldwin's death. Fulk was no stranger to the East. Like his ancestor the Black Count Fulk Nerra, Fulk V had previously travelled to the Middle East. Though it is not recorded exactly when he became initiated into the mysteries of the Knights Templar, the time span of his inauguration into the order undoubtedly covered the period from 1118 to 1128. Fulk's son and heir to the Angevin empire, Geoffrey Plantagenet, had been born in 1110, the product of Fulk's marriage to the daughter of Count Elias. But by 1128 Fulk had lost his wife, leaving him free to marry King Baldwin's daughter.

Fulk then ruled in Jerusalem, leaving Geoffrey to take care of the Angevin territories with the knowledge that Geoffrey's betrothal to Matilda—Henry I's heiress daughter—would bring either Geoffrey Plantagenet or his future son in turn the Kingdom of England.

There are no records of Geoffrey Plantagenet being admitted to the inner sanctum of the Knights Templar, but did his father Fulk V, who was an initiate of the Order, divulge any of its secrets and mysteries to his son? If any such intimate conversations did occur, they would have happened prior to 1129 and Fulk's departure to Jerusalem.

Perhaps one possible clue in this respect lies in the Grand Master of the Order's alleged comment to Geoffrey Plantagenet's son, Henry II of England: 'You shall be king as long as you are just'. Would the Grand Master have delivered such a warning to a monarch with such a volatile temperament as Henry II unless there had been some sort of accord between the monarchy and the order—albeit only through Henry's grandfather being one of its formative members?

Certainly, Henry II maintained close links with the Templars here in England. They were attempting to conciliate the king's position with Thomas à Becket, though this, of course, was to end in disaster and tragedy.

They built their original Temple on the site of what is now Holborn underground station in London, England, before moving to the temple site near the Thames embankment. *Barran Novi Templi*, or Temple Bar, the point where Fleet Street joins up with the Strand, was the gate of the then New Order's precincts, which reached from Aldwych up the Strand along a sizable part of Fleet Street and down to the Victoria Embankment and the Thames, where they had their own wharf. The temple site still contains their original round church plus a number of graves.

By 1161 the Knights Templar were already established on this site, and it was here that a yearly meeting of the general chapter was convened and attended by the Master of England and all other dignitaries of the British order, encompassing also those from Ireland and Scotland. The order expanded at quite a rate, acquiring land, property and wealth all over Europe. Attaining influence and power, the Temple became both feared and revered. King John, who borrowed heavily from its funds, had as his closest adviser Aymeric de St Maur, the Master of England, and it was he who persuaded the king to sign Magna Carta in 1215.

Meanwhile, Henry II's other son, Richard Coeur de Lion, kept the closest links with the Temple. He was granted virtually honorary status among the Templars, and he regularly associated with them.

In France, however, the monarchy became increasingly indignant at the rise of the Templars, issuing orders that all Templars in France be placed under arrest at dawn on Friday October 13, 1307 and that no information concerning the order's rituals was to be circulated.

The Templars were purged, many of them tortured, though it seems they were forewarned of the impending crackdown—their wealth and treasures were never found. Thus the French king's goal of seizing their fortune was never realized. Under the heel of such an inquisition it is not surprising that the Templars were made to confess to all manner of things demonic. These revelations included reports that unapproved witnesses of their rituals had mysteriously disappeared; they were accused of worshipping a dark power called 'Baphomet', and they were also cited for desecrating, trampling and spitting on the Cross, together with other serious crimes of heresy.

Historians remain sceptical as to the validity of the confessions in view of the fact that so many in France were extorted under extreme duress. However, in England the authorities assumed a far more lacklustre position, with many Templars escaping arrest altogether. Yet in June 1311 one Templar, Stephen de Stapelbrugge, was taken prisoner in Salisbury and became the first English Templar to confess to most of the alleged crimes against the Templars in France, the only difference being that Stephen made his statement utterly voluntarily under no apparent threat whatsoever. He also stated that the order's 'errors' had emanated from France, near Agen to be more precise. Blame was firmly laid upon Roncelin de Fos, Master of Provence, who became Master of England in 1251.

It was affirmed by other witnesses that all perverse and evil innovations in the Temple had been inaugurated by a former Master of the Order, Brother Roncelin. As the Agen region had also contained much of the Cathar heresy, it was concluded that the Cathars had subsequently 'infected the Templars with their thoughts'.

But as Fulk V of Jerusalem, Count of Anjou—the man feared above all others by Henry I—was one of the original Templars, and bearing in mind the twisted history of the Angevin dynasty, is it not possible that the Templars were in part tainted from the beginning? It was Fulk's son

Geoffrey who first used the Plantagenet emblem that also linked his line to the Old Worship.

Another historical clue in this respect is provided by the kingdom of Kerak, a god-forsaken place strategically situated on the southeastern edge of the Dead Sea in what is now Jordan. Stephen Howarth's book *The Knights Templar* (1982) refers to a castle of awesome size and appearance, which had been in evidence at Kerak since the 12th century. In the Old Testament, Isaiah the prophet had put a curse on the Kerak community, allegedly because of sacrificial rites and idol adulation. These practices were the type of activities that fostered the Golden Calf legend.

The area where the castle stood was inhabited as long ago as 1200 BC, when Yuya-neb's Dead Sea community was forming at En-gedi. There was then a spilt of communities with opposing ideas, and one community moved from around the west bank and established itself in Kerak. It was a place of importance right from those early times, during the Templar reign and again in the 18th and 19th centuries.

When Bertrand de Blanquefort, the Templar Grand Master, died on 2 January 1169, his successor, Philip de Milly was appointed without delay. De Milly, though of French ancestry, had been born in Palestine. He had control of the fortresses of Kerak and Montreal, and had been made the seventh Master of the Order of the Temple one week after being accepted in the order, the first Palestinian-born lord to achieve such a status.

Jerusalem and parts of the Middle East were ostensibly the Temple's seat of interest, as Europe was only to be a substructure to the main focus of the Temple activities. But in 1187, after repeated assaults by the armies of the Muslim leader Saladin, the eighth Master of the Temple, Gerard de Rideford, lost Jerusalem and with it Kerak and Montreal.

Finally, in March 1314, it seemed that the French monarchy's purge had reached its finale with the roasting alive of Grand Master Jacques de Molay. It was said that when he died he cursed the king and the Pope by condemning them to appear before the Court of God within a year. Both King Philippe and Pope Clement V did in fact die during that same year. Consequently, the French Monarchy felt that it was bedevilled, an affliction that continued through the centuries.

In their book *The Temple and the Lodge* (1989) authors Michael Baigent and Richard Leigh chart the demise of the Templars and their hitherto undiscovered re-emergence in Scotland, where the Templar heritage was to take root before spawning freemasonry from the ashes of the old religious–military order.

The link between freemasonry and the Knights Templar had fascinated historians for many years, with some dismissing as myth any such links, yet in *The Temple and the Lodge* the authors prove the connection through the discovery of old Templar graves in Scotland and architecture bearing Masonic symbols, plus the preservation of Templar traditions by British elite families and others associated in French high circles. The authors also credit the 16th-century alchemist Dr John Dee with setting the stage for the emergence of freemasonry.

The root of the Templars' demise, of course, lay in the allegations made of them by the authorities, which involved their purported worship of Baphomet. There are, however, various definitions of Baphomet, both in the context of the idol itself and its derivation.

First, when the French King's henchmen forced their way into the Parish Temple on Friday October 13, 1307, they discovered a silver reliquary in the shape of a head, which contained a woman's skull. When the Inquisition drew up the charges against the Templars on August 12, 1308, they included items to the effect that in each province the Templars had idols, namely heads which they worshipped. The purpose of this idolatry was to make the land fertile.

These items have also been attributed in Celtic tradition to the Grail romance and the severed head of Bran the Blessed, which was buried just outside London with its face turned towards France as a protective talisman, thus ensuring against any would-be attack as well as the continued fertility of the surrounding land. The Celtic cult of the head affirmed the ancient belief that the soul was contained in the head and that heads of conquered foes should be severed and preserved.

However, there is also another aspect of Baphomet, which involves the Hekate tradition, namely that Templars were said to have worshipped an idol with three faces or sometimes a stuffed human head. Whether a triple aspect or just a singular one is not certain, although the French Inquisition did refer to heads in the plural, and the Templars were accused of believing that the heads were the source of their riches and would bring fertility to the land.

The origins of the name 'Baphomet' remain somewhat of a mystery. It is partially explained by being an alteration of the word 'Mahomet', which was spelt 'Bafomet' in Provence, the centre of the Cathar heresy and which was believed to have influenced the Templars. In fact there is a 'devil in the church' set in the stonework of the church of Saint Merri, France, which is supposed to be the idol Baphomet, worshipped, according to some sources, by the Templars. The idol consists of a head, chest and arms folded around the knees and lower calves, the whole

figure being in a semi-seated or perching position.

Another depiction of Baphomet was discovered on a building that was once in the possession of the Knights Templar—the Commanderie of Saint Bris le Vineux. Here the figure can be seen in the same seated position as the 'devil in the church' at Saint Merri. In other respects the gargoyle is more reminiscent of a popular image of a devil figurine. It has cloven feet, wings and drooping female breasts. Its posture is like that of the old Celtic god of the Underworld, Cernunnos, as portrayed in statues.

However, the image that had become most identified with the Templars' Baphomet, as it was said partly to comprise the Baphomet figure, was Eliphas Levi's 'sabbatic goat', or Baphomet of Mendes (see Chapter 3). Like the Templars' Baphomet and the aforementioned figures that are supposed to represent it, Levi's sabbatical goat appears in a seated position with a torch rising from the top of its head as a symbol of divine revelation. The four elements are contained within the figure, the head generally representing fire; the wings, air; scales, water; and legs, earth. The hands and arms symbolize masculine and feminine aspects: the hands point to a black and white crescent Moon respectively characterizing the lunar phases.

Much of the evidence concerning the Templars points towards them being, in all probability, clandestine Goddess devotees of some sort and much like the Assassins and Sufis before them who were themselves identified as goddess worshippers.

One other aspect of the Templars' mysterious Baphomet is worth mentioning here. The late Madeline Montalban, one of the foremost authorities on the tarot, had defined the Baphomet character as a symbol of the zodiacal sign Capricorn, which in turn signifies the occult image of the goat as well as the material desires of the Templars.

The late Montague Summers (*The Geography of Witchcraft*, 1958) was of the opinion that the Templars were in fact what he called 'gnostic heretics, dualists whose beliefs had developed on the lines of the Luciferians'. He explained this vein of reasoning as follows: 'It must be borne in mind that the Christians in Palestine at the time of the Crusades were often affected by their contact and intercourse with the religious systems of the East, notably with gnostic bodies professing a distorted form of Christianity, as also by their constant intermingling with their Mohammedan neighbours.'

Though the Templars' prime objective had been to unite Europe politically, governing through Christian doctrines, their view of Christianity was almost at odds with that of the Papal priesthood in Rome. The Templars were said to have been enthused by the Egyptian Mysteries believing that their remote ancestors were the ancient Alexandrian gnostics. They could also be ruthless in pursuit of their own objectives. In 1172 Hassin sent representatives on behalf of the Assassins to King Amaury I of Jerusalem with a view to commencing religious negotiations so that the Assassins and their followers could embrace Christianity. But the envoys were not allowed to carry out their commission: they were deliberately murdered by order of the Templars. If the Templars were such avid exponents of Christianity—albeit their own version of the faith—why turn on their allies in such a brutal manner when faced with the prospect of their impending conversion to Christianity?

According to Montague Summers, the 'Assassins actually paid tribute to the Templars'. By this he meant that the Assassins acknowledged a form of submission to them—the obligation to pay tribute. The emissaries of Hassin took with them one precondition to their conversion to Christianity—that the Assassins be released from the bond or tribute they paid to the Templars—and this would be put to the King of Jerusalem as the main part of the bargain.

Summers postulates that the 'Assassins were in some way subordinate to the Mandaeans' whose 'Patriarch Theocletes had invested the Grand Master of the Templars with his right and powers.' Whatever the relationship between these orders was, the Templars obviously felt they would lose their influence or some measure of control over the Assassins if the latter's envoys were allowed to complete their task. Their subsequent elimination showed a cruel pragmatism on the Templars' part, enabling them to maintain a hold over their associates; that was of far greater significance to the Templars than the Assassins' would-be enrolment into the Christian fold. The Templars had shown that they were quite capable of placing their own order's ambitions before any acts of righteous chivalry.

Summers adjudges the worship of the Templars as follows: 'They worshipped not only a Supreme Deity, the Creator of Spirit and all good, yet who was, however, supposed to be unapproachable by man and inaccessible to human understanding, but they also acknowledged another Deity, the Author of Matter and all evil, and him they adored with mystic and peculiar ceremonies.'

Summers was of the view that Baphomet originated from the Greek word *baphmetis*, which translates as 'the baptism of wisdom'. This apparently referred to an arcane ritual to which only the Grand Master of Templars was privy.

Clearly the Templars' occult indulgences were allowed to get out of control, and it seems likely that something similar occurred in the case of

Bishop Henry de Blois of Winchester—in which case he would have played a formidable role in Andrew Collins's hypothetical Dark Council.

The notion of a sinister Dark Council of high churchmen, who were also involved in demonic or gnostic worship, is by no means a new or unique one. Albertus Magnus (1206–80) who became Bishop of Ratisbon in Bavaria, was reputedly a sorcerer-monk. There were also popes who were said to be involved in sorcery. The famous fifth-century pope St Leo the Great, Pope Honorius two centuries later and Pope Silvester II in the 11th century were all considered to be involved in questionable occult practices, with some written magical works being attributed to them.

It was not only high churchmen or secret military orders, however, who were involved in demonic or similar occult practices.

Chapter 8
Secrets of the Realm

We have already looked at the tradition that holds that the Plantagenet kings preferred the Old Religion, with some of them being secretly involved through the lineage of the Angevin dynasty and its shadowy pagan past. However, the same is also true of some in the Norman line of descendancy, notably William II, more commonly known as William Rufus.

In *The God of the Witches* (1962) Margaret Murray chronicles the religious beliefs and death of Rufus, concluding that not only was he an avid apostle of the Old Worship but that he was also ritually murdered because of the position he allegedly held within it.

The whole concept of the Divine King being killed at the end of a specific period in time so that his blood can be used in fertility rites and thus maintain the luxuriance of the land, is one whose origins date back to early history. In old Norse mythology it was at Samhain that the Old Kings were ritually burnt (see Chapter 6). One of Rufus's favourite utterances whenever he was under some kind of threat was 'By the face of Lucca.' Dr Murray believed that Lucca was a variant of Luce or Luci, and that the name referred to a god of some sort, though the nearest I could find in name to Lucca was Lucetia/Lucina, the sister and consort of Jupiter, who was also a Moon goddess and in the latter respect was twinned with Diana.

However, Dr Murray was of the opinion that Lucca was in fact a Latinized version of the Norse demon god Loki—one of the supreme deities of Norse mythology. Dr Murray believes 'By the face of Loki' would be an appropriate oath for a Norseman.

Rufus was more openly an advocate of the Old Religion than any of his Plantagenet counterparts, who tended to be more secretive, almost dualistic, in their displays of religious affection; Rufus was, however, overtly scornful of Christianity, the saints and the apostles. Consequently he was despised by the Christian chronicler-monks, who doubtless contributed to his historical

notoriety, though in practice he compared favourably with most of his peers.

Of the roots of Rufus, Margaret Murray says 'By ancestry, Rufus came of pagan stock which regarded the king as a deity (or devil if the Christian phraseology is used). It is recorded that at the end of the 10th century or beginning of the 11th, the Devil, in the likeness of the Duke of Normandy, came to the duke's wife in a wood, and as the result of the union she bore a son who was known as Robert the Devil.'

Unlike some of his Angevin counterparts, Robert showed no characteristics to provide any grounds for such an epithet. But Dr Murray maintains that the king or chief was regarded as 'God incarnate among the Normans', and that these beliefs were an integral part of the fundamental dogma that was practised in the older, pre-Christian religion of Europe.

The son of Robert the Devil was William I (William the Conqueror), whose marriage to his cousin Matilda bore three children, Robert Curthose, Henry I and William Rufus. The latter became known as the Red King on account of his name Rufus (meaning red)—a colour that was sacred to the Old Religion. The friends and associates of Rufus were of a similar persuasion, and the line of descendancy becomes more pertinent still given that both Rufus's parents were of the same family.

Though there are varied accounts of his death, all versions agree on its exact manner—that he was killed by an arrow fired from one of his own party while out hunting in the New Forest. The conventional viewpoint is that it was an accident, though the whole affair remains one of the great mysteries. According to Dr Murray certain evidence was suppressed by the chroniclers at the time, and in light of this the event takes on a different slant.

The chronicler Knighton's version, as documented in *The God of the Witches* (n. d.), states that Rufus was shooting at a stag when his bowstring snapped, so he called upon Walter Tyrrel to shoot; the latter was reluctant to do so, prompting Rufus to bellow: 'Draw, draw your bow for the Devil's sake and let fly your arrow, or it will be the worse for you!'

Tyrrel did just that, but his arrow misfired and hit the king. In the account given by William of Malmesbury, the King did not speak when the arrow penetrated him. He merely broke off the protruding shaft where it had entered his body and fell upon his injury, which served only to hasten his demise.

Rufus was forewarned of his own death, and there are indications that he knew his end was near even before he received the warning. On that fateful August day, as he and his party were preparing for what was to be the king's last hunt, Rufus was brought six new arrows, two of which he gave to Tyrrel, saying, 'It is right that the sharpest arrows should be given to him who knows how to deal deadly strokes with them.'

At that precise point in time, a written communication arrived from Abbot Serlo, the Norman abbot of St Peter's at Gloucester, appealing to the King not to take part in the hunt because a monk had had a premonition in the form of a complex vision of Christ and the Virgin Mary, warning the King that such an excursion would result in death.

Commenting in his comprehensive and analytical book *The Killing of William Rufus* (1979), Duncan Grinnell-Milne says that this may have been intended as a genuine warning, as whispers of a conspiracy of some sort could have reached Gloucester 'loud enough to alarm the loyal abbot'.

Rufus appeared to laugh off the message and its portent of doom, but he turned to Tyrrel and said, 'Walter, do thou justice according to those things which thou hast heard', to which Tyrrel replied 'So I will, my Lord.'

If the conversations that occurred between these two men are accurate, and the accounts of Rufus's death provided by Dr Murray are true, then not only did the king fully expect his own death to occur, but he also coerced one of his closely trusted confidantes into helping him accomplish it.

Duncan Grinnell-Milne, however, is of the opinion that the conversation between Rufus and Tyrrel actually took place around midday, some six hours or so beforehand—and that the two men were in fact referring to the situation on the Continent and not Serlo's harbinger of the king's demise.

Whatever the exact truth concerning the mysterious death of Rufus, one intriguing fact remains—that his demise was known about as far afield as Italy within hours of its occurrence, and that it was anticipated in some quarters before it actually transpired.

Another significant factor is the date that Rufus was felled by the fateful arrow—August 2, 1100.

The Legend of Lugh

Lammas, celebrated on the first day of August each year, is an important ritual date in the witchcraft calendar. Its history dates to when it was called the Feast of Lugh, or Lughnasadh, when it was one of the four major pre-Christian festivals normally celebrated on July 31, as the August Eve Great Sabbat, in the old pagan calendar.

Lugh was the grandson of the underworld god Balor, who was the most feared of the Fomorii, a race of evil, violent and malformed people who, according to legend, lived in a domain of permanent darkness.

A prophecy had foretold of Balor's death at the hand of his own grandson, so Balor tried to kill the infant by throwing him in the sea, but a druidess had saved the child and looked after him. Lugh became known by several names, translated as 'he of the long hand', 'he of mighty blows'

and 'he of many gifts' because of his expertise with spear and sling; like Odin, his symbols included the raven.

When he was fully grown and skilled in the required arts, Lugh offered his services to Nuada, the ruler of the Tuatha de Danaan, 'the peoples of the goddess Dana', whose sworn enemies were the Fomorii, and during the second Battle of Magh Tuireadh, Nuada was overcome by Balor's evil eye, which emitted such a malicious stare that all who were unfortunate enough to encounter it promptly perished. Lugh, however, assisted by a magic stone ball which penetrated the eye's drooping lid, destroyed Balor, and vanquished the Fomorii, thus fulfilling the old prophecy, and he became a prominent deity in the old Irish sagas as King of the Tuatha de Danaan in Nuada's place.

It seems that this legend may well have fostered the phrase putting the 'evil eye' on someone or something, although the story is very similar to that of the Greek god Perseus, who slew the Gorgon whose gaze turned men to stone.

The Festival of Lugh later became Lammas, or the feast of the first fruits, and was fixed for August 1. The Anglo-Saxon form of Lugh or Lughomass was 'loaf mass' (half mass), and it related to the corn-harvest and the killing of the Corn King.

In *Eight Sabbats for Witches* (*op. cit.*) Janet and Stewart Farrar refer to the triple goddess in her battle aspect, in the form of the Three Machas, as the 'trine patroness of the Lughnasadh festival'. The high priestess invokes the goddess into herself, but defers this process until the death of the holly king.

This of course is the ancient ritual as in the Old Worship, which has the same theme running through it from the Balor/Lugh tradition: the transference of power from the elder god or king to the new one or to the followers or subjects, by virtue of making the land fertile for the people.

In her book *The Divine King in England* (1954) Margaret Murray asserts that the supreme sacrifice made by the king as a willing victim was in fact the real purpose and secret of being king. Hugh Ross Williamson supports Dr Murray's theories, and looks further into the events leading up to the death of Rufus in his book *The Ancient Capital*. On November 1, 1099 a calamitous tidal swell had flooded the North Sea coast and the Thames. This happened on Samhain day, which was seen as a bad omen. In order to appease the gods a divine victim was selected for the ultimate sacrifice. At the beginning of May 1100, the nephew of Rufus was accidentally shot in the New Forest. He was the illegitimate son of William's brother, Robert Curthose, but apparently a bastard royal offspring was inadequate for such an important ritual: it had to be the royal godhead himself who would be offered as the divine victim at the next important sabbat, which would be Lammas.

July 31, or Lammas Eve, is also the night when the Norse god Loki is honoured. If Dr Murray is right and Rufus was a devotee of Loki, his death on August 2 assumes a greater significance. In Norse tradition, July 29 commemorates St Olaf, the Norwegian king who was also killed during Lammas time—though, like Rufus, not necessarily on the actual festival day itself. The previous day, 28, is dedicated to the Irish sacrificial god Domhnach Chrom Dubh—Crom for short. His sacrifice in the older worship was substituted by other human victims who were ritually slain at an altar or phallic stone encompassed by a stone circle containing twelve or a similar number of stones. In later times a bull was used instead of a human in the rites of Crom. The commemoration of Crom is also linked to Lammas, and likewise John Barleycorn, the grain incarnate who is executed by laceration as part of the ancient fertility rite.

The saga of John Barleycorn has been told and retold in numerous versions of the folk song bearing his name, with differing interpretations dating back to the 15th century and said to have originated in the Home Counties area of southern England.

The Lammas festival itself, on July 31/August 1, marks the eighth and last station of the year, a matter of completion before the start of the winter quarter at Samhain; it is sacred to Odin, the Norse rune master and leader of the Wild Hunt in Norse legend.

Did Rufus help bring about his own demise using the symbolism of the Wild Hunt, or at least his own enactment of it? Was it really conceivable that the reigning monarch would involve himself in such an undertaking?

Duncan Grinnell-Milne had no doubts that Rufus was murdered by one of his own hunting party but points the finger of blame squarely upon Rufus's brother Henry, who seized the throne immediately after his brother's death. Henry's only legitimate surviving daughter, Matilda, married Geoffrey Plantagenet, thus combining the pagan houses of Anjou and Normandy.

However, in *The Killing of William Rufus* (*op. cit.*), Grinnell-Milne absolves Tyrrel of any blame whatsoever in the plot with his contention that Tyrrel was actually in another part of the woods away from the king when Rufus was felled by the fateful arrow.

Grinnell-Milne quotes Gerald of Wales, who maintained that the 'King was shot by Renulf de Aquis', which was possibly a Latinized name for a Norman knight-huntsman called Raoul des Aix—a shadowy figure of whom little was known other than that he appeared to be the principal co-ordinator of the king's hunting parties. Being an official of such high standing he was apparently above suspicion in the alleged conspiracy to murder the monarch; according to Grinnell-Milne, Tyrrel was made the scapegoat for the 'accident'.

If Grinnell-Milne's conspiracy hypothesis is correct, casting a leading Norman knight-huntsman as the assassin under orders from Henry, then there was enough Wild Hunt symbolism in the death of Rufus to suggest that the perpetrators were probably aware of the Wild Hunt's significance, especially as Lammas time is sacred to its legendary Norse leader Odin. But the burning question remains: how much did Rufus know?

Perhaps one clue lies in the activities of his father, William I, shortly before the first Norman King's death in 1087. The previous year William had begun to complete his personal matters. On August 1, 1086, he held a council at Salisbury. Present were members of the gentry, landowners of importance. It was said to be a gathering of exceptional size. This event, along with William's behaviour during this year of his life, has confounded conventional historians.

Author Michael Harrison, however, is sure of the reasons. In his book *The Roots of Witchcraft* (1973) he says of William's Lammas council at Salisbury: 'It was Williams's leave-taking of the principal members of the Old Religion. He was due to die in the following year; both he and all the assembled company knew that.'

William I did indeed die the following year—from a mysterious internal injury after he had attacked the French town of Mantes and set it on fire. If William I had entrusted his loyal dignitaries with the news of his forthcoming fate, it is not inconceivable that his son William Rufus would have carried on in the same manner, probably with the hunting entourage, no matter who was actually responsible for firing the lethal arrow.

The violent death of Rufus close to an oak tree in the New Forest has been written into pagan folklore and is symbolized, fittingly, by the line drawing of an arrow.

In *The God of the Witches* Margaret Murray argues that the old pagan calendar with its divisions at May and November Eve and the cross-quarter days at the start of February and August respectively, belongs to a period in time that precedes the introduction of agriculture. She says: 'It has no connection with sowing or reaping, it ignores the solstices and equinoxes, but it marks the opening of the two breeding seasons for animals, both wild and domesticated. It therefore belongs to the hunting and pastoral periods and is in itself an indication of the extreme primitiveness of the cult and points to a very early origin, reaching back possibly to the Palaeolithic era.'

This is obviously another reference to the 'older condition of worship' and the Wild Hunt. At Lammas the triple goddess, or probably her localized form, is invoked, which again brings us back to Hekate, or her localized form, as leader of the Wild Hunt.

If Dr Murray's theories concerning the origins of the four great sabbaths

1. Previous page: *Clapham Woods, North Tunnel.*

2. Above: *Chanctonbury Ring, 1983.*

3. Below: *West Kennet Long Barrow.*

4. Above: *Spiral patterns inside the long barrow. Were these images drawn to signify an energy-harnessing ritual involving rune magic?*

5. Below: *Silbury Hill.*

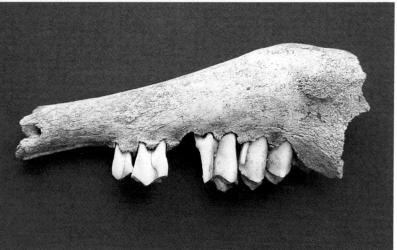

6. Above: *The remnants of St Catherine's Hill as it was being destroyed by the M3 motorway extension in 1994.*

7. Below: *Section of a goat's jawbone, which formed part of a circle found inside the West Kennett Long Barrow.*

8. One of several occult artefacts—a piece of slate inscribed with an ouroboros serpent encircling a Monas *hieroglyphica* symbol—found at Danbury Church, Essex, as part of the 'Black Alchemist' investigation by Andrew Collins.

9. *The demonic mural at the Clapham Manor House complex, an image that* *has now assumed a greater significance than was at first realized.*

10. *The black dagger that pierced an animal heart, unearthed by Andrew Collins at Danbury* *churchyard in 1987. Was this shocking image part of a conceptual Antichrist creation?*

11. The initiation of an 18th-degree Freemason, a Scottish ritual. Note the 'Eliphas Levi' Satanic goat's-head mask, minus the pentagram and the Rosy Cross, on the chest of the lofted figure. Was this Scottish rite part of an earlier tradition passed down by the Knights Templar?

12. The Ritual Killing of Thomas à Becket. His cap is in the form of Mithraic 'Phrygian'. The fatal blow is administered by Sir Reginald Fitz Urse ('son of the bear') whose name discloses him as a devotee of Artemis the bear goddess, who is often twinned with Diana/Hekate.

13. Absolution for the Incarnate God. This shows King Henry II stripped to his undergarments and being ritually punished for ordering Becket's death. The king is being beaten by a cleric using the Plantagenet's birch, or witches' broom.

are correct, the so-called fertility rites actually grew out of a much earlier vein of worship that had more to do with the Wild Hunt than the fertile land.

Doreen Valiente (*op. cit.*) is also of the opinion that the sacrifice of the divine king not only dates back to a much earlier period in history but that it is linked with 'the matriarchal order of primitive times' and the great goddess.

The Divine Substitute

Margaret Murray believed that Thomas à Becket suffered the same fate as Rufus and the other kings, only in Becket's case he was a divine substitute for the reigning monarch, Henry II, she maintained.

Becket was murdered on December 29, 1170—hardly a propitious day in the old pagan calendar, yet as with Rufus, some clerics had dreams and visions of Becket's death, and he himself knew that his end was near and that it would be a brutal one.

William of Canterbury said of Becket, 'He knew that the sword threatened his head, and the time was at hand for his sacrifice'. Despite the warnings from his clerks to the contrary, Becket went about his normal business on the day of his assassination at Canterbury Cathedral, even to the point of instructing that the main church doors should be left open.

When the killing party, comprising four knights, arrived at the cathedral they were able to access the part of church where they knew the archbishop would be. One account published in the *Plantagenet Chronicles* quotes Becket's last words to include these: 'I commend myself and the cause of the Church to the Blessed Mary, the patron saints of this church and the blessed Dionysius'.

The name Dionysius here refers to Dionysius the Areopagite, not the horned Greek God Dionysus. Of Dionysius the Areopagite, little is known other than that his four principal works were written under this pseudonym *c*. AD 500 or possibly earlier; his true identity was never known.

He devised a sequence, still used by occultists, known as the celestial hierarchies. It was a complex series of groups, names and numbers which corresponded to the spiritual sphere of attainment through nine levels descending from God to man and originating from a fusion of Gnosticism and Christianity, and as complex in its structure as the Sephirothic scale of the Jewish cabbala.

Some of the writings of Dionysius the Areopagite reveal a vein of thought that had its roots in Gnosticism, and for Becket to refer to 'the blessed Dionysius' virtually on his own death-bed showed that he could have had secret leanings towards forms of Gnosticism or at least to ideas outside orthodox Christianity.

He was slain by four wounds to the head, which took the form of a virtual ceremonial scalping by the sword. William Fitz Stephen's *Life of Becket* describes how the knights had tried to take him prisoner and drag him out of the church but Becket would not budge from his position, saying 'Here shall you work your will and obey your orders.' He struggled against being abducted from his church but not against his death, freely permitting the fateful blows that severed the top of his head after he had fallen by an altar dedicated to St Benedict.

As with Rufus, Becket's death was known about in several other regions on the very day that it happened and in parts of the West Country at the very moment that it happened.

A state of conflict had existed between Becket and Henry II for some six years prior to the archbishop's climactic and cruel murder. After the last meeting between the two men in Normandy, when the archbishop mounted his horse to depart, Henry clasped the stirrup for Becket while he settled upon his mount.

Margaret Murray saw this gesture of humility by the king as an indication that Becket had consented to be the divine victim or substitute for the king. Henry was not noted for being self-effacing—quite the contrary, he submitted to no one. For him to be seen to kow-tow to Becket in this way was, according to Dr Murray, an acknowledgement that the proper king would temporarily be subservient, albeit symbolically, to the substitute king until the time of the latter's sacrifice by consent.

Two illustrations, both of which appear in Michael Harrison's book *The Roots of Witchcraft* (*op. cit.*), further reinforce Dr Murray's viewpoint. *The Ritual Killing of Thomas Becket* shows precisely that. The tragic archbishop is seen in the foreground of the picture being struck the fatal blow by the sword of Sir Reginald Fitz Urse ('son of the bear') whose name relates to Ursa Minor, the Great Bear, and shows him to be a devotee of the bear-goddess Artemis, herself often twinned with Hekate as Goddess of the Seven Stars. Becket's assassin has a large bear drawn on his shield.

In *Absolution for the Incarnate God* Henry II is seen stripped to his undergarments and being beaten—fittingly by a cleric, who is using a birch or witches' broom—as ritual penance for Becket's murder. The symbolism here is significant: the Plantagenets had taken their name from just such an instrument. Henry had alleged pagan ancestry on both sides of his family tree. Not only was he an Angevin but his mother Matilda was also the daughter of Henry I—brother of and successor to William Rufus.

Margaret Murray's hypothesis on the question of the divine sacrifice is that it occurred once every seven to nine years in Britain and parts of Europe.

She provides several examples as evidence in *The God of the Witches* (*op. cit.*). No real reason is given for such a time span between divine victims other than tradition or that the king's time was up.

However, there is one probable explanation. In Ancient Greece the great year, as we have seen, comprises two denominations of fifty months—one hundred months, or eight and a quarter years. According to Doreen Valiente this was the period when, in the most ancient times, the sacred king was allowed to reign. After this he became the divine sacrifice and his blood was allowed to flow freely on the land as part of the ancient fertility ritual. But as Robert Graves tells us, it is Hekate whose name means 'one hundred' and who is connected to the symbolism of the great year (see Chapter 2).

Therefore it is Hekate to whom the divine victim was offered in the days of the older worship, which, seemingly, has its roots not in fertility rites but even further back in time—in the Wild Hunt.

Order of the Garter

Throughout the history of occult practices, the wearing of a garter was said to be the distinguishing mark, denoting that the wearer possessed occult powers.

Inside a cave at Cogul, in north-eastern Spain, there is a rudimentary painting, which portrays a 'dance of the garter'. In *The God of the Witches* Margaret Murray describes the origins of the Order of the Garter and its alleged links with the occult and royalty.

During a Ball at Windsor Castle given by King Edward III, the garter of his mistress, the Countess of Salisbury, fell off while they were dancing together. The king immediately retrieved the fallen garter and shouted, 'Evil be to he who evil thinks'. This statement was seen by some to signify that the King realized the implications of the countess wearing the garter and was trying to protect her from the possible wrath of his clergy.

By the same token, however, the countess had revealed herself to be the high priestess or queen of an exclusive coven of some sort. Realizing this, Edward III had immediately formed the Order of the Garter in 1348. This order comprised twenty-six knights (or two covens of thirteen). It was dedicated to the Virgin Mary, the Christianized equivalent of the pagan great mother goddess. Meetings of the order occurred In a special chamber inside Windsor Castle around a table that had been fashioned along the same lines as the one used by King Arthur and his Fellowship of the Round Table. The king pronounced himself chief of one of the covens, while he made the Prince of Wales chief of the other.

In Froissart's *Chronicles*, it is stated that Edward III then informed his court

that this new order would prove 'an excellent expedient for the uniting not only of his own people but of all foreigners conjunctively with them in bonds of amity and peace'. In his book *The Devil and All His Works* (1971) Dennis Wheatley seizes upon this statement, saying that it refers to 'the followers of the Old Religion on the Continent'.

Probably because of its insignia, the Order of the Garter has often been associated with the Rosicrucians. The insignia comprises a jewelled collar containing twenty-six gold knots, which alternate with small garters sprouting gold and red roses. It has also been documented that the king's son had links with a group of knights who had been initiated into the Templar tradition.

On their return from the Holy Wars to England, these knights founded an esoteric lodge, which was directly involved in occult practices. Since its formation in 1348 many men who belonged either to the Rosicrucians or the masons have been made members of the Order of the Garter, a title that can only be bestowed upon them by the reigning monarch.

Margaret Murray's theories have been largely dismissed by both the historical and anthropological establishments, yet others, among them Lewis Spence, have supported her. Spence's own researches into witchcraft and the occult had convinced him of the soundness of Dr Murray's views. In summarizing them he wrote:

'She inclines to the hypothesis that witchcraft was in reality the modern and degraded descendant of an ancient nature-religion, the rites of which were actually carried out in deserted places and included child sacrifice and other barbarous customs. In brief her hypothesis tends to prove the actual reality of the witch-religion as against that of hallucination which until recently was the explanation accepted by students of the subject.'

Finally, Stan Gooches highly acclaimed book *Guardians of the Ancient Wisdom* (1979) also supports Dr Murray's contention concerning 'the significance of the Order of the Garter, and her belief that highly placed officials were secretly following the Old Religion'.

Richard III, the last of the Plantagenet kings, cast by Shakespeare as the profligate, carried a notorious banner which showed a white boar. The pig or hog was also a symbol of the lunar goddess known as Hekt, who, in her Germanic form was Hexe and in Greco-Egyptian, Hekate. The curved tusks of the boar are also symbols of the Moon in crescent form, which relates to Hekate.

During the witch trials of the 14th century and the years that followed, many probably innocent people were found guilty and executed; were they in fact scapegoats?

If people in high places were secretly practising the Old Religion or corrupt forms of it, were they able to use their positions in society to escape detection and prosecution at the expense of those not so well placed? Is this a case of the peasants paying the ultimate penalty for the sins of their masters?

Catherine de Medici—Sorceress Monarch

In France, however, Queen Catherine de Medici's involvement in the occult was even more pronounced. The Italian-born daughter of magician Lorenzo de Medici, she married Henry II of France, bearing him three sons—Francis II, Henry III and Charles IX, for whom she was regent. During the reigns of her sons—who all became kings of France—she exercised a powerful political influence. Her appreciation of art and literature was offset by her unscrupulous and cruel nature.

By all accounts, Catherine de Medici was heavily involved in occult practices, being described as a 'sorcerer-monarch' in one account, along with her son, Henry III. She surrounded herself with astrologers, notably Nostradamus, who predicted the death of her husband, Henry II, and a mysterious, questionable occultist called Cosmo Ruggieri. Although this man possessed undoubted skills in astrology, he was also a necromancer and made effective use of the 'waxen doll image' against King Charles IX in 1574.

Cosmo was arrested following reports that he had made a wax image of the king with the intention of harming the monarch by dealing the doll repeated blows to the head. Within a month, Charles IX was struck down by a mysterious consumption and died on May 31, 1574. Sources within the French court believed that the king had been 'fatally enchanted by the Protestant sorcerers', who had on a daily basis melted waxen images representing the monarch; this had gradually sapped his strength and life force.

Catherine de Medici's devotion to the occult science continued right up until her death, aged 72, in 1589 at Blois. This was the place that had given Bishop of Winchester, Henry de Blois, his name. The elder brother of both Henry and King Stephen de Blois was Theobald, Count of Blois, who had inherited the title from their father.

Catherine de Medici was also in possession of a magic talisman, which she carried with her always. It was originally designed by the Sieur Regnier, an infamous mathematician/sorcerer to whom Catherine had dedicated the building of an astrological column at the Hotel de Soissons in 1572.

The talisman was discovered after her death. It had been broken, but has since been reproduced—painstakingly engraved with the exact facets of the original, which itself is now preserved in the Cabinet of the Abbé Furvel. According to the French occult writer Emile Grillot de Givry (*Illustrated Anthology of Sorcery, Magic and Alchemy*, 1991), the reproduction engraving is unique, and with only one genuine copy of the original in existence, very few people have actually seen it.

The talisman has two faces, one of which contains the jackal-headed Egyptian god Anubis holding a mirror to Jupiter, who is seated on his throne accompanied by the eagle of Ganymede and various symbols representing aspects of Jupiter. The other side is of particular interest. At the top is the word HAGIEL in bold capitals. This was the name according to the 'Intelligency of Venus' by the 16th-century German occultist Cornelius Agrippa, based on ancient cabbalistic sources. The naked Venus figure below is said to represent Catherine de Medici herself. At the bottom of the talisman are the words NANIEL EBVLEB (Beelzebub) and ASMODEI.

In Agrippa's work Faust is said to have made his pact with Beelzebub. *The Grand Grimoire* and *Grimorium Verum*, two 18th-century magical textbooks, declare Beelzebub to be part of the 'supreme trinity of evil', along with Astaroth and Lucifer.

S. L. Macgregor Mathers, co-founder of the hugely influential Order of the Golden Dawn, said that when attempting to invoke Beelzebub the magic circle must be properly drawn and the preparation completely accurate. Failure to observe these guidelines could easily result in the immediate death of the operator.

When summoned by the magician, Beelzebub materializes in the form of a huge fly. This symbolic imagery dates back to the ninth century BC, when the demon of Ekron, a Philistine city situated to the west of Jerusalem, was originally called Baal-zebub ('lord of the flies').

In the *Book of Black Magic* (1989) former master of the Golden Dawn A. E. Waite gives an account of the conjuration of Satan in the name of Beelzbuth. This is contained in the grimoire called *The Method of Honorius*, and described by Waite as 'perhaps the most frankly diabolical of all the rituals connected with black magic'.

The Grimoire of Honorius first appeared in the 14th century, but apparently derives from the works of Solomon—though not from the *Grand Clavicle* or 'Key of Solomon' itself.

Asmodei (Asmoday), whose name appears engraved at the bottom of Catherine de Medici's talisman, is one of seventy-two demons' names in the *Lesser Key of Solomon the King*. This text, also known as the *Lemegeton*, is a work of pure demonic magic regarded as one of the definitive grimoires by 17th-century occultists. The seventy-two demons named are portrayed as dangerous dukes or many-headed warriors, some of which are part man, part animal.

Asmoday is described in the *Lemegeton* as being a powerful king with three heads, those of a bull, a man and a ram. He has a serpent's tail and webbed feet, and vomits fire. He is the chief of the power of Amaymon (the demon king of the eastern regions of hell) and appears carrying lance and pennon, and riding an infernal dragon.

According to occult historian Fred Gettings (*op. cit.*), Beelzebub is actually the leader of this entire demonic ensemble, though he is not mentioned anywhere in the text of the *Lemegeton*.

Also visible on Catherine de Medici's talisman are various seals and symbols, which also relate to the images and words inscribed. The talisman was said originally to be a compound of human blood, goat's blood and various metals melted together under certain constellations, which are linked to Catherine de Medici. It was asserted that the talisman's virtue was for sovereign governance and future knowledge.

Author Peter Haining credits the creation of the black mass to Catherine de Medici. She had devised a reverse blasphemous mass—that of the Catholic Church read backwards—which was performed at ritual ceremonies. In his book *Witchcraft and Black Magic* (1971) Haining describes Catherine de Medici as 'a woman of licentious and depraved tastes—she was drawn to the darker elements of the occult, then very widespread in Europe.'

After Catherine's husband Henry II of France died, her preoccupation with the pursuit of occult science led her to accumulate a select court ensemble containing some unseemly people—notably the sinister Cosmo Ruggieri and Nostradamus. She was soon introducing noblemen and others in high places to the black mass, even involving her own young sons. According to Peter Haining, 'this was to have far-reaching effects both at home and abroad in the centuries to come'.

Realizing that to reveal too much of the truth could cost him his head, Nostradamus was careful in what he disclosed to the formidable sorcerer-monarch in the form of predictions. He explained to her that he had no control over his visions—he only registered events as they appeared to him. Nostradamus had amassed a collection of rare occult books and manuscripts whose contents he relied upon for his knowledge. In particular he had been influenced by some dark magical texts, which he later decided to burn as they had conflicted with his strongly held religious principles and beliefs. He wrote:

Many occult volumes which have been hidden for centuries have come in to my possession, but after reading them, dreading what might happen if they

should fall into the wrong hands, I presented them to Vulcan, and as the fire devoured them, the flames licking the air shot forth an unaccustomed brightness, clearer than natural flame, like the flash from an explosive powder, casting a peculiar illumination all over the house, as if it were wrapped in sudden conflagration. So that you might not in the future be tempted to search for the perfect transmutation, lunar or solar, or for incorruptible metals hidden under the earth or sea, I reduced them to ashes.

This statement provides us with the clearest indication that he was fully aware of the people in 'high places' who were involved in questionable occult practices and the dire consequences should his rare collection fall into the wrong hands.

Catherine de Medici's involvement was mainly with what is known as ritual or ceremonial magic (see Chapter 3) as opposed to aspects of the Old Religion. The black mass, which she has been credited with establishing, is mainly the reversal of the Christian Catholic mass into a libation to Satan. This tended to take the form of a collection of rites rather than one particular ritual. The first known black mass was held in the seventh century, according to occult writers J. Tondriau and Roland Villeneuve (*A Dictionary of Devils and Demons*, 1972). This is earlier than first thought, but in fact its origins may well date from an even earlier time.

Pagans and witches will readily point out that the black mass is not part of authentic witchcraft or pagan practices even though the popular concept is to the contrary. However, in the book *Witches Still Live* (1931) by Theda Kenyon I found an intriguing reference to the origins and practice of the black mass in the chapter bearing that title. The author says, 'From the earliest days of Christianity, the members of the pagan cult, the rising witch cult, mockingly imitated every rite and custom of the new faith. They could hardly have avoided imitating the mass; and when we discover that in the eighth century Egbert, Archbishop of York, forbade offerings to devils, it seems that the cult had already thought of the 'sacrifice' and put it into practice.' She goes on to say: 'If the mass pleased the new deity why not the old? It would have been strange indeed if the mass to the Devil awaited discovery by some savant of the middle ages.'

The clear implication here is that while we consider witchcraft and satanism to be different there is quite probably a crossover point in some cases, combining the two veins of worship together. While many pagans became involved in non-sacrificial nature worship, did some witch-cult members move in the opposite direction?

Mary had suggested as much when she said that it was the 'reversal of the signs' that the Friends of Hekate had been practising in their rituals.

But how far back did this method go? The first example of sign reversal in this manner was in all probability the inverted pentagram, or pentagram of Kali Yuga, which was believed by some to have been in use during the last days of Atlantis—its implementation by the corrupt sorcerers apparently being instrumental in the cataclysmic downfall of the once supreme continent before its subsequent use by elements within the Zoroastrian priesthood, which ultimately led to their fall from grace.

One of the main protagonists responsible for perverting the cult of Zoroaster was its one-time leader Sardanapalus, who, over 2000 years ago, was the King of Nineveh (in what is now the supposed safe haven for Kurds in northern Iraq who have fled the tyrannical rule of Saddam Hussein). Sardanapalus, much like his 20th-century counterpart, was cruel and implacable, and revelled in his abuse of power. Under his rule the high principles of the Zoroastrian magi had been allowed to fall into a cesspit of sorcery, until the remaining masters who had refused to succumb to the condition of reversal within their priesthoods, could no longer tolerate the ruination of their once-great religion.

The masters had one final ace to play, which they used to devastating effect. They not only understood all the secrets of fire and the power that could be obtained from its use, they also apparently knew about electricity in its most primitive form. This was their final mystery: it was said to be the power at their command, which they could manifest in the form of artificial lightning using methods that are, even today, outside our field of knowledge.

Sardanapalus also knew of it and had tried to exploit it for his own gain, but the magi were more skilful, and it was Sardanapalus who was obliterated in a storm of artificial lightning. But he had been the king—the godhead of the cult of Zoroaster—if only for a short time, and as such he became the first recorded victim of the divine sacrifice.

Whatever the exact truth about his death, the responsibility was laid firmly at the feet of the avenging Zoroaster priesthood's inner sanctum.

The secrets of Zoroaster became lost in the centuries that followed: fragments of the knowledge became embodied into other mystery cults and travelled westwards, having an undoubted influence upon other secret sects for generations to come. However, the remnants of the cult of Zoroaster held their mysteries, too. For centuries people came and saw the craggy carved images of the lion and the snake without being aware of their significance. The lion signified the sun, while the serpent was said to represent that last great Zoroastrian mystery—the power of electricity and self-manifested forms of artificial lightning. But secrets such as these

probably died with the Zoroastrian Hierophants of that era, while the practitioners of the Dark Worship can only tinker and experiment with such forces.

Other symbols, too, contained their own wealth of secrets—notably the mysterious Hekate Wheel, with all its grades and protective Serpents—but there was yet more to come in connection with the wheel and the groups that were related to it.

Chapter 9

The Wheel-based Conspiracy

Wheels Within Wheels

'The Wheel' was a term Andrew Collins had first come across in 1981 when his psychic colleague Graham Phillips had used it to describe what he understood to be a sinister worldwide organization derived from the medieval Knights Templar.

Prior to the order's savage purging by the authorities at the beginning of the 1300s, the Knights Templar had amassed vast wealth and riches in the form of land and financial control of the treasury systems of various European countries. They had become virtually all powerful.

During the first of my interviews in 1982 with Mary, the psychic consultant, she had referred to the 'spokes of the Roman wheel' merely as a metaphorical term symbolizing the ancient alignments of the arcane energy matrix in relation to the activities of the Friends of Hekate. She had never mentioned the wheel in direct relation to any conspiratorial organization, so the assertions of Andrew's team were all the more interesting in this respect.

In his book *The Seventh Sword* (1991) Andrew Collins charts the history of an extremely arcane organization, apparently in existence since the fall of the Templars, and known simply as 'The Wheel'.

Its members are apparently an 'opposite force', operating as wheels within wheels—tiny but powerful cogs turning and operating other much larger concerns, and have permeated every facet of society throughout Europe. It seems quite possible that they have taken their name from the sixth-century BC illustration discovered by Charles Walker called *The Hekate Wheel*.

One of Andrew's multi-talented team of psychic researchers for *The Seventh Sword* made this chilling proclamation concerning 'The Wheel' and

107

its activities: 'They are much more than an organization as you would know it. They have been the power behind some of the most atrocious acts of mankind, and they still exist today. In years to come you will learn much of them. You will confront them face to face and they will oppose you.'

'The Wheel' has had several influential representatives down the centuries who have succeeded in thwarting attempts by others to appropriate the key to real occult power by practising dark rites themselves: anyone who has confronted The Wheel has come to an untimely demise, and *The Seventh Sword* cites examples of these.

Much of the unpublished material Andrew had amassed on The Wheel reads like a document on world conspiracies, and must therefore remain unpublished in order to avoid the numerous libel suits that would be bound to follow if it ever saw the light day. However, Deborah Benstead, another of Andrew's team, believed that its tentacles stretched worldwide, sucking into and attempting to control levels of religion, business, politics and the military. On an occult level it wanted to dominate the ancient magical systems of countries, and was trying to achieve this here in Britain. By taking over the natural energy matrix, The Wheel will turn the key to real occult power over the country's material and spiritual destiny.

Andrew firmly indicates that it was events at Kerak—the old kingdom once positioned on the south-eastern edge of the Dead Sea in what is now Jordan and cursed by the prophet Isaiah in the Old Testament (see Chapter 7)—that nurtured what later became The Wheel.

The Middle East was, in effect, a spiritual power-base for the early Templars. They were linked to the sect of Mandaeans, also known as the Johanites, whose patriarch Theocletes, the sixty-seventh successor of the apostle St John, invested his knowledge and powers in Hugues de Payens, the first Grand Master of the Templars in 1118.

Von Hund and the Hidden Masters

It was in France during the 18th century, however, that many new lodges of a rogue Scottish variety were inaugurated. They appropriated both Rose Croix and Templar rituals, including those supposedly attached to the Royal Order of Scotland and ordained by Robert the Bruce after the Battle of Bannockburn in 1314. In fact the Royal Order of Scotland claimed direct heredity from the Knights Templar,, and during their time of continental self-exile, they set up these new lodges in France and Italy. These in turn helped create the most significant of all the European Scottish Templar organizations—the Rite of the Strict Observance, instituted by Karl Goffhelf, Baron von Hund, in 1751.

Some nine years prior to this, von Hund had been made a third-degree master mason of a Frankfurt-based lodge at the age of twenty. He had then travelled to Paris, where he was contacted by Scottish Rite Templar masons who wanted to initiate him into their inner secrets.

This duly occurred the following year and in the presence of such dignitaries as Lord Kilmarnock and Lord Clifford. However, the final ritual act of acceptance into the Scottish Templar order was carried out by a hooded, robed and masked figure revealed only as the Knight of the Red Feather.

Masonic disclosures were made to von Hund concerning Scottish freemasonry and its Templar origins, and he was assured that there would be further substantial information forthcoming to him when the time was right, at a future date. He was told that Scots masonry was established all over the Continent, and that he was to be the head of its seventh province, covering Germany. After a secret visit to Scotland in 1751, von Hund returned to Germany with the prerogative to instigate the Rite of the Strict Observance. This meant that all initiates or 'brothers' must pledge their strict obedience to the inner order's arcane Unknown Superiors (Superiores Incogniti), whose real identities had not been revealed even to von Hund.

In 1772 Hund was retired to an honorary position. He had always maintained that his supposed Unknown Superiors were unidentifiable. He was replaced by Duke Ferdinand of Brunswick, who became the new Great Superior. The Duke sent an emissary to try and unmask the order's faceless masters, and, based on information received, the emissary went to Florence. On returning he reported to the duke that he had witnessed initiates conjuring ghostly spirits in the presence of Charles Edward Stuart (Bonnie Prince Charlie), the self-exiled Pretender to the British throne. The emissary had asked Charles if he was indeed the Grand Master of the Strict Observance and consequently one of the Order's Unknown Superiors. The Young Pretender denied all knowledge of any such secret order.

More was to come. Information was passed to the emissary from those in the confidence of the Pretender, which linked the order's Unknown Superiors with seven monks who worked in one to the seven caves beneath the Servite monastery deep in the Tuscan countryside.

The Servite Order was a strict religious community founded on the peak of Monte Senario in 1593, but it had been suppressed a year after Bonnie Prince Charlie established himself in Florence. It is worth stressing here that Charles Stuart was of Catholic stock, and initiates of the Strict

Observance Order were expected to adhere to the same faith, albeit sometimes only in a token vein. Like Guy Fawkes and the gunpowder plotters, the Jacobites and Charles Stuart wanted to overthrow the government of the day and reinstate Catholicism.

But the Duke of Brunswick did not share the opinions of his emissary, and in 1782 at a major conference for European freemasons near Hesse in Germany, he denounced claims of a direct descendancy from the Knights Templar as 'unjustifiable', and disbanded the Order of Strict Observance. In his book *The Seventh Sword*, however, Andrew Collins postulates on the linkage between Bonnie Prince Charlie, Scots Templarism, the Strict Observance and the Tuscany monks. He writes:

'Was it possible that ascetic monks from the monastery of Monte Senario had acted as spiritual advisers or Unknown Superiors to Charles Edward Stuart and his masonic associates? Despite Prince Charles's official response to the Duke of Brunswick's emissary, there was ample evidence to show that the Young Pretender had indeed been the Sovereign Grand Master of Scottish Rite Masonry. There also seemed little doubt that he and his colleagues had been the unknown Superiors of their German brothers in von Hund's Strict Observance.

This much seemed obvious. However, was it remotely possible that the Servite monks held some key to the original concept of the Seven Swords of Meonia? Their use of the seven swords to represent the Seven Sorrows of Mary was strangely coincidental, if nothing else. Perhaps they had been aware of some ancient ritualistic event, which they saw in terms of seven swords coming together symbolically to pierce the heart of Mary? If so, had they related this to the Second Coming, the return of the Agnus Dei, the Lamb of Revelation, which was the emblem of office for both the medieval Knights Templar and the 18th-century Scots Templar masons?

'Could the monks have listened in earnest to the prophecies of the Scots Templars, which spoke of an approaching new epoch of the Holy Spirit, and then have given them the formula to achieve both their spiritual and political aims? This would, of course, have included the collapse of the Hanoverian kings of Britain, the restoration of the Stuart monarchy and the reintroduction of Catholicism as the state religion.'

If this were the case, then it is likely that the formula discussed between the Templars and the monks involved the casting of seven swords and the instigation of a Catholic-based masonic rite, which exists today as the 'Form of the Lamb'.

The ritual involving the initiation of the Knights Templar priest is of particular interest. According to *Beyond the Craft* (1980) by Keith B.

Jackson, this rite begins with passages from the Old and New Testaments being read aloud. The candidate is taken to seven 'pillar officers' who hold seven swords while standing in front of seven pillars placed in a triangular alignment. Each of the pillars is engraved with a word, which betokens one of the seven attributes of the Agnus Dei, the Lamb of God, who opens the seven seals to reveal the disparate spirits of God.

Another rite involves the bearing of seven swords by seven knights, who also bear an insignia in the guise of a seven-pointed star pendant.

Both Templar 'degrees' have a heredity whose origins are founded in the continental 18th-century Scottish Rite freemasons. The unity between the Scottish Stuarts and their French counterparts was symbolized by the monogram designed by Mary Queen of Scots to portray her love for her first husband, Francis II of France. This appeared on the cross-piece of the seven Meonia Swords—though the first of these was not apparently cast until 1772, some 78 years after Mary's death, and disappeared during the 1770s after being held by Hund's Strict Observance. The swords reappeared at different locations and times from the 1970s onwards, and were apparently brought together in central England in 1992 for a secret ritual known as the Form of the Lamb.

The Ordre du Temple And The Black Sword

During 18th century some fairly sinister individuals began to form their own Templar-based groups constituted from the fragments of the Strict Observance and the like. One of these self-promoted high priests was a mysterious, shadowy adept of Portuguese–Jewish extraction called Martines de Pasqually.

Born in 1700, Pasqually had travelled the Middle East in his early years and become influenced by the cabbala and goetic magic. The Wheel had apparently recognized Pasqually's potential and taken him to Castle Kerak, on the Jordanian side of the Dead Sea, and initiated him into a highly secretive Rose Croix organization.

In 1754 Pasqually had formed a ritualistic occult order called the Rite of the Elect Cohens (*Elus Coens* or the 'chosen priests'). Membership was available only to third-degree craft freemasons. The higher degrees of the Rite of the Elect Cohens culminated in a clandestine Rose Cross degree. They practised deviate forms of cabbalistic rites. Elect Cohen's lodges soon appeared in Bordeaux, Marseilles, Toulouse and finally in Paris in 1768. Before he died in 1779, Pasqually himself wrote four books, *Proteus*, *Axioms*, *The World* and *The Wheel*.

It is believed that one of the 18th-century Meonia Swords had been appropriated by the Elect Cohens, who realized its importance after the downfall of the Strict Observance. This sword, known as the Black Sword, then fell into the domain of what Andrew Collins believed was a similar wheel-based Templar organization called the Ordre du Temple, which was closely linked to the Elect Cohens. This assumption was confirmed by occult historian Francis King, who stated that Pasqually's teachings had influenced the foundation of the Ordre du Temple.

The Ordre du Temple was originated by a freemason called Bernard Raymond Fabre-Palaprat. Palaprat was also pontiff of a weird pseudo-Catholic Christian sect which believed in the power of the three Johns— the Baptist, the Evangelist and the Divine. They also believed that Jesus had been fathered by a demon called Pandira or Panther. This movement was called the Johannite Church, and was, in actuality, a public façade obscuring a far more malevolent organization called the Société de l'Aloyou, or the Society of the Lion.

This organization was rooted in medieval templarism and debauched freemasonry, and was known to be in existence up to the period of the French Revolution. It was after Fabre-Palaprat had been promoted to the rank of pontiff that he announced publicly that he was in possession of a genuine document known as the 'Larmenius Charter', which bestowed upon him the right to inaugurate a Templar resurgence.

The document declared that before his execution in 1314, Templar Grand Master Jacques de Molay left specific instructions for the continuation of the order. To succeed himself as Grand Master he had nominated John Mark Larmenius, a Palestinian-born Templar from Cyprus, who duly became the next Grand Master ten years after Jacques' execution in 1324; from him had emanated a perpetual line of Grand Masters through the centuries to this particular period.

In fact, though the Larmenius Charter was first made public in 1804, its existence had previously been acknowledged some 99 years before, in 1705.

The Ordre du Temple conducted its affairs in total secrecy, and by all accounts practised everything that their accursed predecessors were put to death for. They followed the warped Johannite Church dogma: they worshipped the demonic form known as Baphomet, because of the word association between the Baptiser of Wisdom and John the Baptist.

It was through these 18th-century Templar revivalist orders and subsequent ones such as the sinister Saviours of Louis XVII, that the overlap between unorthodox freemasonry, the Rose Cross (or Croix Rite) and demonic practices occurs. The belief in a prophet or demon for the new

epoch—the Second Coming in the form of the Lamb of Revelation—
would have instigated the creation of such sinister orders, which would
have kept the evil eye firmly on the manipulation and appropriation of any
such sacrosanct notions for their own ends.

The Eighteenth Degree

The first appearance of Levi's Sabbatical Goat of Mendes in 1856 must have
seemed like a demonic bequest to these orders, who adopted its imagery
into their own Rose Cross Rite. It is the fusion of Scots Templar masons and
French demonic occultism that is being displayed in an illustration showing
a so-called 18th-degree Scottish rite that had also been adopted by
schismatic masonic orders.

The illustration depicts Scottish Templar masons carrying the hoisted
figure of what, in posture and appearance, resembles almost precisely
Eliphas Levi's Baphomet or Goat of Mendes, save for the pentagram, which
is missing from the forehead, and the insertion of the rose inside the cross
worn on the chest.

In 1889 Eliphas Levi founded a new Rosicrucian society called the
Cabbalistic Order of the Rosy Cross. This group was set up in direct
opposition to freemasonry. Levi, together with his associates, insisted
that the new order should be elitist, open only to Catholic initiates,
much like the orders that had preceded it—a move that would be in
accord with Scottish Templar masons sympathetic towards the values of
the Stuart tradition.

In England the 18th degree is known as 'Knight of the Pelican and Eagle
and Sovereign Prince Rose Croix of Heredom' and marks the end of an
initiated first hand of progression in craft freemasonry. Beyond this point
the number of initiated diminish (up to and including the 33rd degree), as
no initiate can rise higher than the 18th degree without the unanimous
agreement of the entire Supreme Council.

The pentacle represents intelligence, according to Levi, and its absence
from the figure's head in the illustration perhaps denotes that the initiate
needs to ascend further before he can be considered whole. Despite the
name 'Rose Croix' being incorporated into the 18th-degree title, the order
itself had no jurisdiction over the majority of English masons, who were not
part of it.

The origins of the Rosy Cross can be traced back to Ancient Egypt, to
the 15th century BC, to be precise. Pharaoh Thothmes III had apparently
formed the original Order of the Rosy Cross, which comprised a secret
priesthood who conducted their rituals in a temple on the banks of the

River Nile. Its aim was to safeguard the Mysteries.

Because of their respective use of the rose emblem, and the son of Edward III's links with a Templar-based group of knights involved in occult practices, the Order of the Garter was connected to the Rosicrucians (see Chapter 8). The Rosicrucians and the Templars both have the red or rosy cross as a symbol within their orders. As Michael Howard comments in *The Occult Conspiracy* (1989): 'Both groups while nominally Christian, seem to have been secretly engaged in occult and pagan practices under the cover of orthodoxy.'

One of the supposed Grand Masters of the Rosicrucian Order was the astrologer and adviser to Elizabeth I Dr John Dee, who has been credited by authors Michael Baigent and Richard Leigh (*The Temple and the Lodge*, 1989) as 'setting the stage for the emergence of freemasonry'.

Perhaps the most significant magical work undertaken by Dee was his Enochian Evocation, which he performed with Edward Kelly. They believed that the true art of magic would alter the European political order, provide the magical operators with untold occult powers and be the harbinger of the Apocalypse. Dee felt that only through the working of magic could these things be attained.

Dee was not involved in the Dark Worship, and rejected the practices and practitioners of the black arts. Nonetheless his fanaticism in pursuing the path of what he called Enochian magic, which was not dissimilar to that of the gnostic texts, in the end led to his downfall. Dee was stretching Kelly to the limit of his prowess and beyond, compelling him to work magical rituals, sometimes for several hours at a time and on a virtually daily basis. In the end both men were fortunate to emerge with their minds largely intact.

As for the Templars, like the gnostics their modes of worship tended to vary from order to order and from temple to temple—a fact not lost in the astute appraisal of Montague Summers. He says:

'It is, I think, idle to deny that the charges made against the order were in the main well founded, but it must also be acknowledged that the degree of culpability varied in different branches, and the majority of members of certain preceptories may have been to some extent ignorant of these transgressions against faith and morals, the secret and genuine doctrine of the Templars not having been communicated to them in its entirety.'

In *Guardians of the Ancient Wisdom* (1979) Stan Gooch broadens the canvas of worship in his conclusions, which are that 'all secret societies with ancient traditions (like the Rosicrucians and the freemasons) were, and are, so far as they are guarding anything, guarding fragments of the knowledge of the old Moon worship. Here we include also the Knights Templar proper.'

Hexing the Matrix

Besides their infiltration into some Templar centres, notably at Castle Kerak in the Middle East, the Wheel's sphere of influence here in Britain lay in their ambitions to appropriate spiritual power or any form of occult power in their pursuit of commandeering the country's natural energy matrix— or so Andrew Collins's team believed. The team was of the opinion that this would apparently be achieved by a force of clandestine covenant, with two main occult organizations in the United Kingdom, who would also be able to draw upon virtually limitless reprises in order to carry out their dark arcane rites.

The first of these groups was a particularly sinister order known as the People of Hexe—taken from the Prussian form of Hekate—and Hexe is, of course, a name meaning 'magical spell'.

The People of Hexe were adepts of a profoundly sinister order with a central three, similar to the former Friends of Hekate. The Hexe triad, who were all of Mediterranean origin, were involved in the resurgence of ancient deities associated with the negative side of British history and mythology. They were appropriating these raw energies by ritual means and acuminating them at power sites or in artefacts.

These artefacts would take the form either of a stone engraved with magical symbols, a piece of bone, or a charged crystal. By executing malign rites in this manner they would be endeavouring to take command of the complete energy matrix of Britain, a slow process that involves constructing their own geometric interpretation of the matrix.

They were also involved, like the Friends of Hekate, in the appropriation of ley power emanating from sites linked with Arbor Low in the Peak District. They were, apparently, basing their ideas on the minotaur and the spider goddess Arachne.

The second of these groups was the modern-day equivalent of the Dark Council, or reformed Friends of Hekate, whose hierarchy were allegedly carrying out corrupt magical rites at sanctified sites.

Andrew Collins sums up the operational methods of this wheel-based group in his book *The Seventh Sword* (*op. cit.*) as follows:

'Its members would take these instructions to their own individual groups of high initiates, telling them that they would have to conduct a specific action at a designated time and place. This they would carry out, knowing only that the direction came from the 'hidden masters' and that it formed part of the great work.

The individual initiates would, in their turn, quite possibly have their own magical groups who, through them, would likewise be instructed to assemble at certain dates and locations in order to conduct rituals as part of an overall plan of events.

It was a complex, confusing hierarchical system which would result in very few people actually knowing what was going on or who was behind the covert operations.'

In other words, Andrew was describing a more involved and wider form of the malefic power spiral used by several high diabolical magical orders throughout the ages, and quite likely by the former Friends of Hekate (see Chapter 1).

The Coming of Ragnarok

Hexe, however, were after any kind of ancient symbolism that they could get their hands on—the darker and bloodier, the better, Debbie had asserted. She believed that Hexe were financially involved with a multinational business conglomerate with several companies in the UK. Some of these business associates were not only pursing power and complete control of the material facets; they were, apparently, the 'main spokes of the Wheel's influence in Britain', while others were not involved in the occult side themselves.

On an occult level, Hexe and those associated with them, were attempting to harness extremely potent forces, using ancient Germanic and Norse god symbolism, among others, in their rites.

Fenris, or Fenrir, was of profound importance in this respect, according to Debbie. In Germanic mythology, Fenrir was a giant wolf who would rise up at Ragnarok and swallow the sun and bite the Moon, before expiring in the final annihilation. The time of Ragnarok is perceived by many to be the equivalent of Judgement Day or the Apocalypse.

Ragnarok in Germanic mythology refers to a period at the end of time when there is a mighty battle. Out of the destruction will come a new order. Andrew Collins and his team are not the only researchers into this theme to have come to virtually the same conclusion.

In *The Mark of the Beast* (1990) Tim Wallace-Murphy has this to say on the same subject matter:

'An international occult lodge is secretly at work in the heart of the financial world which spreads its malign influence throughout the political and economic structures of the entire planet. Total control of the political machinery of all parties is sought by infiltrating and financing not only the majority of candidates from all sides, but also by the provision of economic advisers to governments. The tentacles of such an international occult circle reach into the intelligence systems and the media, into education, science and the military.'

In *The Black Art*, published in 1936, the Egyptian magician and author Rollo Ahmed also said: 'On the Continent, if not in England, there are black magic centres whose aim is political and financial intrigue.' Ahmed, a lecturer and practitioner of raja yoga, had studied the black arts, travelling to many countries. He had also met and conversed with white magicians, and such was his understanding of all magic that he was held in the highest esteem by the likes of authors Dennis Wheatley and Doreen Valiente.

Fenrir, or the Fenris wolf, is the progeny of the Scandinavian god of subterranean fire, Loki, who can be directly linked to Satan. With the coming of Christianity, many of the old Norse gods had become demonized and Loki's many evil deeds had meant that this fate would also befall the 'arch deceiver', as Loki had become known. Both Loki and Saturn became identified with Satan.

In *The Pedigree of the Devil* by Frederic T. Hall (1883), I found an interesting reference to Loki, which reads: 'Beelzebub, Lucifer, Loki, Set and the Deuce have each in his time sat high among the gods, and as they all must be ranked as ancestors of the modern devil, it may fairly, and indeed literally, be said that Satan has fallen from Heaven.'

Andrew Collins had mused that if the son of Satan is the Antichrist, the spawn of Loki (Fenrir) could be seen as a Norse interpretation of the great beast, one of the forms of the Antichrist. In fact, the whole saga of Fenrir/Fenris and Ragnarok could be easily equated with the predicted coming of the Antichrist, particularly in the minds of those who were set on utilizing the symbolic power of Fenrir and twisting the outcome of Ragnarok for their own ends.

The pieces of animal bone used by Hexe in their rituals had been signed by the group in the form of a pentagon inside a hexagon and placed beneath the ground as a concealed fixing marker, symbolizing their interpretation of the energy matrix and its alignments.

Mary had first drawn my attention to the Friends of Hekate's ambitions in this respect during my interviews with her back in 1982.

The People of Hexe—the modern day Dark Council—were probably only tenuously connected by virtue of all being under the black umbrella of the wheel. Yet collectively the energies generated by their individual corrupt ritual activities would provide the impetus for the process of attaining total spiritual control, which would subtly slip into the grasp of

the wheel over a period of time.

That time was, apparently, fast approaching. The year 2000 and the first decade of the new millennium have been seen by many as a spiritually critical period in our history.

The planetary alignment that virtually matches the earthly arrangement of the planetary sites where the druidic oracles were originally placed, and where seven cathedrals stand, occurred in May 2000 (see Chapter 5). This plan of alignments is said to mark the apocalypse in stone form (as revealed in *The Mark of the Beast* by Tim Wallace-Murphy).

The stonemasons who erected the pillars at Rosslyn Chapel in Scotland—one of the centres in the alignment—were aware of its significance. Those involved in the Wheel are aware of it too. They intended to have the Wheel of occult power grasped firmly in their hands by, or shortly after, the turn of the millennium. That was the aim of their alleged conspiracy.

Chapter 10

The Horns of
the Dilemma

The material concerning the Wheel and its operations was falling into place and beginning to make some sense, but there were still crucial aspects of the Dark Worship that required further in-depth scrutiny if I was ever going to find the complete picture.

I had been looking at some material that Charles had previously researched from *The Witches' Goddess* (*op. cit.*) by Janet and Stewart Farrar in relation to St Catherine. He had discovered that when the Nigerian sister goddesses Oshun and Oyo had been taken by slaves to Brazil, they had become voodoo goddesses identified with St Barbara and St Catherine (see Chapter 6). Oshun (spelt *Oxun* in Brazilian) is patroness of the zodiacal sign Capricorn.

While reading through this material, Charles had been reminded that in the very earliest days of Babylonian symbolism Capricorn was a horned goat with a mermaid-like tail. The Greek astrological tradition depicts this creature with a twist in its tail. When various sources referred to scales on the body and a horned creature, the demonic mural, which Charles had photographed in Clapham back in 1979, immediately came to mind.

I had previously concluded that the demonic mural was a grotesque depiction of Hekate that was singular to the group. Andrew Collins, too, felt that it was probably a representation of the high priestess's allegiance to the goddess in some form or another. But there was nothing on view that symbolized the triple goddess. Hekate, of course, comes in different and varying forms; the image still posed somewhat of a dilemma, however.

I recalled asking Mary in 1984 exactly what the demonic mural was and what precisely she made of it. After I had shown her the colour enlargement of the photograph, she had said:

'It is one of the goat—although they call themselves the Friends of Hekate, it's all the same thing; there's no difference because everything is done in reverse. Though you have the priestess you came back to the Moon and the horns. They [the Friends of Hekate] only use the positions and conjunctions of the stars. All the light we get is reflected. They—the stars—have been dead for a long time now. The power is in the atmosphere partly, and the Moon and the planets are more influential than the stars in this respect.'

Mary's description of the demonic mural certainly verified Charles's Capricorn material. Early medieval manuscripts depicted a form of Capricorn that was near to the Babylonian horned goat with a mermaid-like tail. However, a little further on in the middle ages the astrological image embodied the more customary Greek definition.

The fusion of a goat and a fish had much inner meaning. The curious combination is reflective of the Capricornian disposition. In the astrological tradition, Capricorn is ambitious and seeking to get to the top of his chosen profession. In the more positive sense Capricorn endeavours to exist in the light of day. But on the down side, Capricorn's fish tail is said to represent the fear in his nature, the shoal in which the individual becomes swallowed up and thereby loses his independent identity.

In a much wider vein, this symbolism reflects the constant struggle currently taking place in various countries, and with the environment and the planet as a whole. Man is at present doing his utmost to detach himself from the tribal instinct (represented by the fish tail) and its requirements, which suppress his individuality. It also struck me, however, that the negative, fear side of this symbolism is precisely what the Dark Council/Friends of Hekate were attempting to achieve. A case of 'if you can't beat them, join them'.

The ancient legends of the zodiac describe Capricorn as being the son of Pan, the god who had the feet and legs of a goat. Capricorn's mother was the divine goat Amaltheia, who suckled the infant Zeus. Here, too, Capricorn is frequently displayed as half man, half goat with a fish's tail—the interpretation being that when the gods were defending their empire against the Titans, Capricorn made a trumpet out of a conch-shell; the awesome noise generated by the instrument terrified the Titans into retreat, and Capricorn was duly rewarded with the tail of a fish.

The Occult Connection

Capricorn is in fact frequently identified with the nature spirit Pan himself. Pan was the god of flocks and fields. When he was attacked by the monster Typhoon on the banks of the River Nile, Pan promptly changed himself into a huge goat with the rear of a fish, and in this form took refuge in the river.

Many demons are shown with horns and cloven feet. One suggestion as to their origin is that the horns are symbolic of the crescent Moon phase and the old belief that the demons occupied the space between the Moon and the Earth.

The Hors of Dilema

The 'lunar sphere' was in effect the darkest level of the 'astral plane'.

According to occult historian Fred Gettings (*Dictionary of Demons*, 1988), 'the horns of the Devil were really the outer symbol which linked the Devil, and the thinking of the Devil, with the Moon'.

In the Book of Revelation the vilest of virtually all the demons was the beast with seven heads and ten horns, which emanated from the bottomless pit.

During the middle ages several representations of the Devil implied a direct link between the Devil-demons and the ancient image of Pan which depicts a cloven hoofed half-man, half-goat creature blowing an elongated trumpet or horn to summon the witches to the sabbat.

Elymas, the Brighton high priest, who had always provided Charles with pertinent advice and information over the years, said that it was Capricorn's links with Pan together with the goat-like image that made this quite a common representation in certain occult rituals.

Sometimes the image would be used in pictorial form, often impossible to distinguish from the traditional goat image usually associated with the dark side of occultism, and occasionally just as the astrological character. Either of these interpretations is quite often used, and Elymas was somewhat surprised that neither Charles nor I had come across it before in one form or another, but the fact remained that neither of us had.

From what Elymas had been able to learn it is the goat-fish part of Capricorn's image that is used to represent fear, at least in occult circles, and not the rear segment of the fish or mermaid's tail. However, taking the image as a whole, Elymas said, 'if you look at most of the goat-fish images of Capricorn, you will notice the rather fierce expression. In the right circumstances, if used properly, that would instil fear in anyone,' he continued. Elymas felt sure that people such as Aleister Crowley and others like him must have used this image or 'tuned into' the facets, influences and traits of Capricorn during their rituals.

Elymas also suggested that it was indeed partly a Capricornian-type image that had influenced the conception and production of the demonic mural at Clapham, though this was not necessarily supposed solely to represent Capricorn—only a facet of it. Although the demonic mural no longer exists, since extensive refurbishments were carried out on the Manor House complex at Clapham, Elymas still gets a 'nasty feeling' when looking at the photograph of it. In fact he feels strongly that there is some 'long-lasting influence' suggested by the image, which had yet to be fully felt. He was unable to pin it down exactly or to be more explicit about the feeling it engendered, but it was one of acute disquiet.

The image is certainly unique, with its facet of Capricorn depicted by the horns and scaly fishtail, and the bald head and feminine face representative of the

Dark Goddess Hekate's symbolism, which was unique to the Friends of Hekate.

Like Elymas, Mary, Bernard and Debbie had all voiced similar opinions as to the build-up of occult forces by the suspect rituals of the wheel-based orders, the full impact of which was yet to be realized.

The Destructive Kronos

In view of Mary's repeated assertions, however, concerning the Friends of Hekate's use of stellar conjunctions and astrological symbolism, I decided there was more to the astrological facet of Capricorn that needed looking at. Fortunately, I was recommended to read Liz Greene's *The Astrology of Fate (op. cit.)*, in which I was able to find precisely what I had been searching for. Like many historians of myth, Robert Graves cites Amaltheia—the Cretan goat goddess who suckled the infant Zeus when Rhea was hiding him from Kronos— as the original goat-fish, mother of Capricorn.

However, according to Liz Greene it is Kronos who is the old goat god of fertility in both Teutonic and Greek myth, associated with the grain harvest. Amaltheia, then, is seen as the succouring goat that gives life to the infants, while on the other hand Kronos is the destructive goat that devours its own young.

When Zeus became Lord of the Universe, he rewarded Amaltheia by placing her image amid the stars as Capricorn. He acquired one of her horns, which was known as the Horn of Plenty, constantly replenished with its keeper's wants. This mythical imagery is synonymous with the Grail legend. But, like the occult itself, there is a positive and a negative side to the Capricorn goat myth—one face of the daimon, Kronos, destroys, while the other face, Amaltheia, gives life.

In *The Astrology of Fate* Liz Greene describes this peculiar combination by saying that there is 'a profound collusion between the dark and light aspects of the same deity. The Terrible Father, who seeks to destroy his son secretly and unconsciously, also offers him salvation through the feminine aspect of the same emblem, which he himself wears. It is this secret collusion which is quite awesome to meet in analytic work.'

In fact the author also chronicles a myth linked to the goatfish, which is more ancient than that of Kronos and Amaltheia. The primordial figure of the Sumerian water god, Ea, whose image is the fish-tailed goat and whose name later converted into Oannes, in Greek. Oannes then became John, which author Liz Greene interprets as the mythical figure of John the Baptist who prophesies the coming of the Redeemer. However, the reverse, negative side of this mythical imagery is of the coming of the Antichrist, as predicted by St John in the Book of Revelation.

In accounts provided by Homer and Hesiod, the planet is allotted two Titans, namely Kronos and Rhea, whose father was Ouranos. After the two Titans had been banished because of their ugliness, Kronos was persuaded to attack his father Ouranos, which he did with a flint sickle—the emblem of the Moon and the power of the goddess. In his left hand Kronos gripped his father's genitalia and promptly chopped them off, casting them into the ocean while the blood from the wound spilled onto Gaia, the earth. Gaia and Rhea are both said to be the same goddess denoting the earth's fertility.

According to Robert Graves, Kronos and the ritual sickle are images that are affiliated with the ritual sacrifice of the king. Saturn, the Roman equivalent of Kronos, carried a billhook that was similar to a crow's bill. The word *Kronos* means time, but it also betokens 'crow' as well. The crow was considered to contain the spirit of a sacrificed sacred king. Often associated with dark occult rites, the crow is also linked to Hekate and 'the crone' as in 'the old crone witch'.

The ritual sickle used by Kronos indicated that the sacrificial death that would in turn fertilize the earth was imminent. Liz Greene also attributes the theme of the fertility rites sacrifice of the old king as 'an ancient motif', which she 'relates particularly to the sign of Capricorn in which the father is the earth itself'.

The ancient King Kronos will devour his own young in order to prevent them from bestowing upon him the same fate Kronos himself inflicted on his own father.

In this, one of the earliest accounts of Capricorn and Kronos, the ancient fertility rites of course relate to the yearly cycle and the full turning of the wheel. They also symbolize a 'very old condition of worship'—quite probably the same as Mary envisaged when she was referring to the Friends of Hekate.

In all probability we could now safely conclude that the demonic mural was in fact a combined image incorporating a facet of Capricorn, embodying the negative destructive elements of Kronos together with the feminine aspects of Hekate that were singular to the Friends of Hekate themselves.

The Influence of Saturn

Saturn is, of course, the planetary ruler of Capricorn. Talismans for Saturn have been found among other occult sigils at Glastonbury, West Kennett and Horsham. The planetary influence of Saturn had also cropped up during Andrew Collins's run-ins with the Black Alchemist and his female accomplice in the autumn of 1987. The sigil for Saturn had been inscribed on the ape dagger found beneath the roots of the hurricane-damaged tree in Danbury churchyard in November 1987. The full Moon symbol had also been found in the same artefact.

Carole Smith, an astrologer friend of Andrew's, had interpreted the symbols,

which were etched into the black blade in astrological terms as the 'Moon conjunct Saturn'. The aspects associated with this are darkness, sorrow, coldness—generally a very bleak influence which is often symbolized by an ageing crone: Hekate, in her crone aspect.

'As a planetary influence, Saturn can relate to the manifestation of things. And the full Moon is very much associated with the completion of pregnancy and childbirth. Combining this full Moon influence with the Moon/Saturn conjunction would crystallize a force or influence symbolized by an old, sterile, yet pregnant hag giving birth, almost against the laws of nature.' Carole had recounted all this to Andrew during the awesome events of autumn 1987, which, in view of what we now know, seemed even more significant.

Mary had also spoken of planetary conjunctions in relation to the timing of the Friends of Hekate's ritual meetings. However, Carole considered that as far as the ape dagger incident was concerned, an attempt had been made to invoke the same aspect or influence of the conjunction by magical instead of astrological means.

Other aspects of Saturn are concerned with ageing and time. The old image of Saturn originates from Kronos, which also means 'time', as we have previously said. The curved knife, which is held by Saturn, relates to the idea of Old Father Time's scythe, the more ancient counterpart of which is the ritual sickle of Kronos.

As a roman deity, Saturn ruled over the harvest and displayed a far more cordial character than in the Greek interpretation. And as a fertility god, Saturn was worshipped by the Romans during December, their Saturnalia coinciding with our Christmas—or more precisely from December 17 to the 23. But this is also a time of the year when the sun is at its weakest point, with the winter solstice on December 21, when the whole northern hemisphere is at its darkest. There is no growth. The ground is petrified barrenness and death is everywhere.

In *The Black Art* (*op. cit.*) Rollo Ahmed defines the Roman Saturnalia as 'one of the earliest forerunners of black festivals.' In Norse myth, with the coming of Christianity, Saturn became duly demonized and was associated with Satan or the Devil along with Loki (see Chapter 9).

But in Greek mythology Saturn is a much more awesome figure, displaying an intense dual aspect that is more profound in its extremes and opposites than any other Greek god-figure. Liz Greene describes it as such in *The Astrology of Fate*: 'Saturn is both pernicious and truthful, bounteous and stingy, terrible and merciful.' She defines the negative aspect of the Saturn/Capricorn link as follows: 'Saturn is the terrible earth father, and his devouring and destroying face, his jealousy and paranoia and power-lust provoke the experience of guilt and sin which seems to be so embedded in Capricorn's psychology.'

The Horns of Dilema

Some astrologers, however, see Saturn, this dark tester, as an essentially feminine influence. An account given by Arnobius in *The Goddess Hekate* (1992) edited by Stephen Ronan, states that Hekate was the mother of Saturn (see Chapter 2), and this appraisal could well explain any feminine influence.

In *The Black Arts* (1969) Richard Cavendish gives an account, taken from the *Key of Solomon* and *True Black Magic*, which provides the planetary influences required for various types of magical procedure. Saturn is suspicious for 'works of death, destruction of injury, raising souls from hell and obtaining knowledge. A waning Moon is favourable to works of hatred and discord. The Moon when almost obscured favours operations of death and destruction, and also becoming invisible.' The waning Moon which Richard Cavendish refers to, is, of course, the time when it is also most favourable for magicians to invoke Hekate: the sign they use is a crescent Moon with three vertical points, two at each end and one in the middle. Those aspects of Saturn's influence in magic quoted by Cavendish of course consist of the negative side in its most extreme form.

We already know that the zodiacal sign of Capricorn is ruled by the planet Saturn, but in the Old Religion the northern deity associated with both of them is Loki—the father of Fenris, a probable Norse interpretation of the great beast, one of the forms of the Antichrist. Incidentally, the animal associated with Capricorn/Saturn/Loki is the goat.

The goat, Capricornus, is also the beast of the Egyptian tarot and is represented by the Devil (number fifteen in the pack) or Baphomet, as in the Templars' infamous idol. Capricorn is also linked to Kali because the goat is sacred to Kali in the Tantric tradition, and her talisman is blood, according to Kenneth Grant. In *Cults of the Shadow* (1975) he refers to the 'fivefold principle', the celebrated Five M's—Makara, which also betokens a fish. Grant explains that this is, in fact, 'the mythological analogue of the zodiacal sea-goat, Capricorn, and as such, specifies the nature of the five M's. These are the five elements, earth, air, fire, water and spirit. They also relate to the pentagram whose number, of course, is also five, and which is associated with feminine aspects.'

In his *Encyclopedia of the Occult (op. cit.)* Fred Gettings links the talisman of the inverted pentagram with Venus. This appears to be in a planetary sense, as apparently a pentagram can be drawn in the skies surrounding the Earth when certain patterns of conjunctions between Venus and the Sun occur over particular periods. Venus is, of course, in Roman mythology, the goddess of love and of spring—hardly a deity to be associated with the symbolism of the inverted pentagram.

However, with Kali the Black the connection is much more relevant. The goat, which is sacred to Kali, forms an image that can be perfectly placed (as a

graphic image) inside the inverted pentagram, or pentagram of Kali Yuga, as it is known. Kali Yuga is the fourth and final Yuga in a compiled time sequence of Yugas, the previous ones being Krita, Treat and Dvapara, which depict a continuing degeneration from an early Golden Age into a much darker one (see Chapter 3).

Besides the name of the goddess Kali being used in respect of these definitions, there is also a pertinent link to Hekate. The sacred emblem of the Kali worshippers (the thuggee) was the pickaxe in the shape of a sickle or scythe. Both the Assassins and the Sufis are believed to be linked with ancient goddess worship through their use of the double axe emblem (see Chapter 7).

Hekate's sigil is, of course, the crescent Moon, which is also the ritual sickle of Chronos and Saturn's billhook. In *Cults of the Shadow* Kenneth Grant talks about the 'sickle-shaped emblem' as being the solar origin of the great mother goddess, as well as Saturn. 'The mother was the cleaver or cutter, she who divided herself in twain as mother and son', Grant says.

These then were the symbols that threaded together the origins and worship of Hekate. Capricornus, Saturn, Kali, the Assassins, the Sufis and probably the Templars too, bearing in mind that one definition of their infamous Baphomet described it as a glyph of Capricorn, another that it was an idol displaying feminine aspects.

According to astrologers, Capricorn is not only the sign of authority, it is also the ~~astrological sign for England itself~~. ARIES

But if these ancient symbols were being utilized by today's corrupt practitioners of the Dark Worship for their own purposes, was there a further link to their method of applying them?

The Numerical Key to Power

Andrew Collins's psychic team had told of a 'national matrix of holy sites being utilised by the Friends of Hekate/Dark Council' with particular reference to 'an arrangement of locations in a huge figure of eight, with St Catherine's Hill acting as a hub of the wheel and Ide Hill forming some kind of starting point'.

Looking at a detailed map of southern England, I tried to mark out a relevant line that would create a figure of eight across the southern and western landscapes by linking up all the other sites known to us, together with St Catherine's and Ide Hills. The results were somewhat inconsistent. Some alignments worked, while others just wouldn't fit into the figure eight frame. There had to be another way of looking at it. Possibly a series of figure eights each aspected differently, some perhaps imperfect? A figure of eight consists, of course, of two perfectly drawn rings. Mary, in naming possible sites that the Friends of Hekate were interested in, had referred to these ancient locations as being 'on the ring'.

I had often wondered about this particular term; now, it seemed, some ten years later, I finally had an answer. Mary wasn't referring to just one ring—she was speaking of two or possibly more. But a figure eight, in her eyes—and most people's—would be seen as a singular complete numerical delineation; hence 'the ring' would be thought of as being 'continuous' as it forms the figure eight. Perhaps she was also referring to a secret system of routes and alignments that had lain hidden for centuries which formed a figure eight across the landscape, but as she was no longer alive there was no way of telling for sure.

What was certain, however, was the fact that the number eight had cropped up repeatedly in our investigations. I researched into numerology, and the various references to the number eight all cited its links the planet Saturn. I had no doubts that this was the final link in the chain. The number eight is also associated with the Caduceus, the magical symbol of Mercury.

Andrew Collins and his team had already found the links between Mercury and the number eight in connection with the affairs of the Friends of Hekate at St Catherine's Hill, Winchester. St Catherine and St Mercury both share the same feast day, November 25, but now we had the undisputed link between the number eight and Saturn.

The ancient mathematicians held magic number squares in high esteem, building ritual centres and other temples on the basis of geometrical designs that occurred within the fabric of the squares. It was a complex system; each of the Seven Wonders of the Ancient World were created on this basis.

According to Eliphas Levi, the Temple of Solomon was itself built on the square of Saturn, yet another example of the magical potency of the Saturn link. Eight also relates to time cycles—the solstices, equinoxes and cross-quarter days. The eight major sabbats are personified by an eight-spoked wheel representing the yearly cycle.

The ancients held a strong conviction that sound was a force of considerable potency which could be utilized for either constructive or destructive purposes. Specific words, sounds and music were used by the early religious practitioners for invocations in which vibration and pitch played a vital role in the outcome of any particular conjuration.

Sounds and words can both be related to numbers. Many ancient doctrines and religions embody numbers in a symbolic manner. Written passages and whole chapters in ancient manuscripts can be decoded numerically to reveal some form of arcane meaning known only to the select few. This method of gematria was used in both the Old and New Testaments.

The figure eight is also thought to symbolize the union of heaven and earth. It is also associated with Rhea—one of the two Titans of Saturn (the other being

Kronos)—and the Cabiri, who were accredited in Lewis Spence's *The Mysteries of Britain* (*op. cit.*) as being the 'ministers of Hekate'.

This added further weight to our link between Hekate, Saturn/Kronos, the facet of Capricorn and the number eight. The number, like so much that we had researched, has a dual nature—which is fairly self-evident from its graphic image, comprising, as it does, two rings.

In the book *Discover Numerology* (1992) by Julia Line, the author says of the figure eight: 'Complete reversals are always a possibility with this number'. This statement provided us with another clue as to why the Dark Council/Friends of Hekate were using it for their own purposes.

Mary had always maintained that their particular practice of the 'old condition of worship' was all about 'the reversal of the signs' and the reversal of everything that was positive. The graphic construction of the figure eight means that it can be reversed without anyone knowing the difference—a disguised reversal, but with a potentially devastating result.

I began to wonder if the wheel-based groups were using the figure eight as some sort of projected psychic imprint, thus bringing about their vision of the personification of power across the energy matrix. If they were as skilful as we had been led to believe, then it is possible that they could realize their objectives psychically by means of visualization techniques. From what we had understood of them, that would certainly make sense. Their apocalyptic vision involved a wanton scavenging of the Ancient Wisdom before mercilessly twisting it for their own destructive aims.

According to occult tradition, a group of adepts concentrating intensely on an image can make it take on a 'thought form', the energy from which can be accommodated to power specific rituals. This, undoubtedly, would be the technique used by the wheel-based groups in their quest to gain control of the country's energy matrix by first interfering with, then appropriating, its sanctified sites.

The key to the whole matter was their quest for energy control, and in this respect we were all aware of the gradual but concentrated build-up of energies that was continuing to take place at many ancient and holy sites across the country.

How could they be stopped? Was there anyone or any group who possessed the necessary knowledge and ability and was willing to try to cleanse the sites that had been previously worked over by the corrupt magical operators of the wheel-based groups?

Chapter 11

Ring of Darkness

Amanda's Vision—August 8, 1993

Anne was in the process of conducting what, for her, was a normal meditation. It was a rather solitary affair, which had found her sitting at home in a quiet space and at an equally quiet moment in time. Everything appeared to be proceeding as usual, but on this occasion she linked psychically into Chanctonbury Ring, only to be met by an overwhelming, seemingly impenetrable black presence. It was as though someone had plopped a solid wedge of black watercolour paint into a bowl of clear water, turning it pitch black within seconds.

Such was its intensity that Anne felt it unwise to concentrate on Chanctonbury any more by herself, so she withdrew from her psychic link to this ring of darkness back into the physical safety of her own sitting room.

The meditation and healing group that she was part of had previously used a strategy that involved visiting a site they had earmarked to be cleansed prior to psychically linking in to its characteristics, before returning finally to cleanse it of negative energies. The first stage of this process was due to happen the next day, but at the allotted time too few members had turned up, and Chanctonbury Ring had to be aborted.

Anne had decided to go back to Amanda's house. They were the two most prominent members within the healing group, and as such they decided to conduct a joint psychic link into the exact nature of Chanctonbury's energies.

At that stage, Anne had not revealed her previous night's experiences to Amanda, as she did not want the pair of them to entertain any preconceived ideas concerning what they were about to participate in.

It was an essentially private session in Amanda's healing room. She had used a large white candle as part of the meditation to symbolize the power of light and a large piece of amethyst crystal to aid the channelling process but at the same time provide protection and enhance their psychic awareness.

At 12 noon they started to link psychically to the Ring. During the onset of their meditation, Amanda had attempted to visualize an extensive light column emanating from the centre of the Ring and rising vertically, but there was something blocking her projected image: she could feel herself travelling astrally over Chanctonbury, only to be met by an intense black nebula, which began to surround her.

She withdrew from the visualization for a few moments in order to gather and recharge her energies, but on re-establishing the link she became aware of a baleful presence in her healing room which began to form into the same dark cloud that had nearly engulfed her a few moments previously—only this time it had permeated into the heart of her healing base.

The blackness had centred around the large white candle. Amanda began to open up mentally to the negative material that had seeped into her sacrosanct room and thus face this nebulous intruder head on. As this course of action progressed, Amanda's visualization moved once more to focus on the ring.

She saw a solemn group of people ascending the hill in a strange circling motion, carrying torches as they twisted and turned, moving towards the summit but in a circuitous manner. Amanda felt that there was a strong female connection and a link to fire. In fact, she was able to envisage a huge cleansing bonfire centred over the amethyst crystal in her healing room, which had purified it from the dark mass. Their meditation link to Chanctonbury at an end, both women were able to reflect on what they had just experienced, and it was only at this juncture that Anne told Amanda what had happened to her the previous night.

Neither of them had ever experienced anything like it before—it was by far the most disturbing fifteen minutes they had gone through during a meditation. Neither of them had read or had any previous knowledge of witchcraft or the occult, so Amanda's vision of the solemn procession encircling the hilltop was even more intriguing.

What she had seen corresponded to the Dance of the Wheel being performed at one of the major festivals in the old calendar, which was linked to goddess worship and fire—aspects she could not have possibly known about. It also reminded me of participants ascending the spiral path of the Lammas hill during the August 1 feast day, which was fitting as Amanda had witnessed the vision on August 9, just a week or so after.

But I felt that she was picking up on something that had occurred a long time ago rather than in the more recent past of such as the Friends of Hekate/Dark Council. Mary had said that while the Friends of Hekate had used Chanctonbury Ring, it wasn't quite right for them, though the site itself did have its roots in 'some devilish goings on'.

For their part, the meditation group had become aware, through some of their members who were alternative health and healing therapists, that negative energies were being emitted from ancient sites in the area because of the corrupt ritualistic activities that were being carried out there, though they had no idea what exactly these rites were. They just knew that the energy balance was out of kilter, and that this was having a diverse effect on the surrounding area generally.

The only way to nullify the iniquitous work of the corrupt occultists, they believed, was to heal the sites, change and redress the energy balance. With careful planning, a little faith and the right approach, it could work.

The Saxon Cemetery

Before tackling Chanctonbury, which would undoubtedly provide them with their sternest test to date, the group had decided to undertake a similar type of meditation but with a smaller group of people, just four persons, at Highdown.

This is an ancient Sussex site situated on downland some two miles south of Clapham and several hundred yards to the north of the busy A259 road. On the top of Highdown Hill itself is an old Saxon cemetery dating back to the fifth century, which forms part of this isolated ridge. At its highest point the hill reaches 266 feet above sea level, but the cemetery and nearby chalkpit remain somewhat concealed by their position and by a clump of trees.

The Saxons who first occupied the site lived at Highdown and introduced their own religion to the area: primeval Germanic paganism. They worshipped gods such as Thunor and Woden, whom they would have invoked immediately prior to departing from their native Germany to southern England. Spear or sword and fire symbolism played a prominent role in their burial rites. The Highdown cemetery contains hundreds of graves, and the extensive discoveries made there have been significant enough for the site to be designated as an Ancient Monument.

Among the finds unearthed from the burial site is a goblet bearing an inscription in Greek. It is believed to have been made *c*. AD 400 in Alexandria, Egypt, a centre of gnostic worship.

But in southern England during the 1980s and 1990s, it was worship of a different kind that was allegedly happening at Highdown. Robed figures had been spotted in the chalk pits at the site by midnight walkers who were alarmed at what they saw: some of the sightings had involved the use of sword and fire symbolism by the participants. There were also reports that those involved had been carrying crosses of fire similar to those used

in the ceremonies of the Ku-Klux Klan in the USA, and this had greatly disturbed the witnesses.

Understandably, it was with a little trepidation that the four members of the healing group carried out their meditation at the Highdown site at dusk on September 17. An eerie stillness had descended on the ancient place as the group's members began their concentrated thought processes. After two minutes, however, they were disturbed by a large flock of crows, which had flown out of the trees and right over the group. A strange wind had also sprung up from nowhere, it had seemed, and started to increase as their meditation progressed, thus giving the whole ambience an aura of disquiet. They were glad to conclude the meditation after an uncomfortable fifteen minutes had passed. Still, it had been a good precursor to the Chanctonbury meeting, which would provide a greater test for the group's abilities.

The Conquest of Chanctonbury

October 24, 1993. At approximately 12 noon twelve people gathered at the summit of Chanctonbury Ring with a view to carrying out their largest and probably most difficult group healing session to date. I had agreed to take part after both Anne and Amanda had asked me to.

Everything, from the timing of our arrival to the exact numbers of persons participating, had been pre-planned in accordance with the objectives of the gathering. Twelve was an important number in this instance. It was, the group believed, the number of people required to change the energies of this ancient hill-fort site. Like seven, twelve is a number that relates to completeness, as it refers to the months or the zodiacal signs that go to make up the yearly cycle. But there was more than just a yearly span segmented into months involved here. Since 1987 the planet had been undergoing a period of almost unprecedented change, economically, politically and environmentally.

The changes were also marked by some extreme weather conditions and climatic shifts. In England the beginning of 1987 saw some record low temperatures, which were accompanied by heavy falls of snow. Then, in October of that same year, the first storm for 300 years to embrace mean speed winds of hurricane force, with gusts of 115 mph, tore devastatingly across south-eastern England. Its power and symbolism had figured in the rites of some corrupt occult adepts including such as the Black Alchemist and the Friends of Hekate who, recognizing the potency of its force and the symbolism of the aftermath, had attempted to utilize those aspects for their nefarious purposes.

On the economic front, the stock-market crash known as Black Friday occurred during the same period as the storm. But these changes heralded only the beginning of a decade or so of conflicts and upheavals—which had been forecast by astrologers some time beforehand; they had pointed towards the conjunction of Uranus–Neptune as being of significance in this respect.

This conjunction is, apparently, a quite rare event, occurring only once roughly every 170 years. However, uniquely, three such conjunctions were set to happen during 1993—the first on February 2, the second on August 19/20 and finally on October 24/25, which would coincide with our visit to the Ring. The final one in this trilogy was probably the most significant, as the earth's energies needed to be altered in order to reverse the negative forces, and it needed to be done by October 25. Otherwise, with Samhain looming and the strong probability that some corrupt occultists would be using the considerable psychic energies that would be around during that time for their negative purposes, everything would go downhill. The moment would be lost. It was then or never, the group believed.

As we walked around what remained of the tree cluster after the storms of 1987 and 1990 had ripped into the Ring, we couldn't help noticing that those trees that remained had grown away from the centre, at strangely oblique angles, in an almost symbolical gesture. It was in the Ring's central area that paranormal and disturbing phenomena had occurred over the preceding years.

While we searched for a suitable spot to begin the psychic meditation I was reminded of one particular incident that had taken place here nearly thirty years earlier. In June 1966, following a report they had read in a local library, four people decided to partake in an all-night vigil inside Chanctonbury Ring. It was around the summer solstice period, so when they arrived at about 9.30 pm the diminishing light of the sinking sun was still strong enough to ensure acceptable visibility for the many people who were continuing to pass by the Ring along the South Downs Way footpath. But as time passed, these other Chanctonbury visitors soon disappeared, leaving just the four overnighters within the Ring.

The atmosphere became very quiet and still as the blazing red sun finally descended below the horizon, marking a perfect end to a perfect summer's day. After a while a gang of motorcycle riders turned up, and as the four investigators had built a campfire in the centre of the Ring, they stayed and chatted for a while before moving away to a further part of the Ring.

Night advanced; all was quiet. At 11.30 pm one of the group, Dave, thought it expedient to make a circle of protection, which he did with powdered chalk, incense and holy water. Once sealed, the group of four then sat within the circle.

Shortly after midnight they heard a kind of crackling noise, distant at first, but becoming louder and then accompanied by a strong, gusting wind, although outside the circle of trees it was still: it was a clear, calm summer's night, and there hadn't, until that moment, been even a breath of wind. The phenomenon lasted about half an hour, and when it ceased a sense of calm returned to the party of four—albeit only temporarily, for at approximately 12.45 am they observed an energy form moving outside the ring of trees. Then suddenly they heard a woman wailing as if in pain, followed almost immediately by the sound of a baby crying, and all the time these things were happening they were aware of the terrifying spectre of the form going continuously around the outside of the trees.

This continued for about forty-five minutes and then the form was no longer to be seen and another somewhat false period of calm descended upon the Ring, lasting for about half an hour. Out of the blue, around 2 am, they heard the sound of a church organ playing accompanied by some form of chanting, and during this period each member of the group felt intense pressure from outside their circle of protection, as if something was trying to penetrate it. Fortunately no one panicked, and after a while these sensations subsided, but at about 2.30 am the motorcyclists suddenly came running through the trees saying they'd experienced something 'really evil' on the other side of the Ring where they'd encamped for the night. All were absolutely petrified, saying they'd never come up the Ring again, and they promptly got on their machines and rode off.

In their rush to leave, the bikers never divulged to the investigators what they had actually encountered. The investigation group themselves stayed until dawn, each one suffering head and body pains, which ceased once they had left the Ring. None ever wanted to repeat the experience.

Bearing all these events in mind, and coupled with the apparent importance of the astrological conjunctions, it seemed that we were carrying quite a weight upon our shoulders as we sat down, having found an appropriate area to the north of the Ring, to commence the meditation.

Anne's idea was to arrange us in a circle of alternating males and females, then to link hands and thus create an energy field within the circle of male plus female energies that we would use to help heal this ancient site. Anne tried with a little difficulty to light three large white candles that had been placed among the roots of a beech tree around which we were seated. Finally she succeeded after finding a sheltered spot away from the north-easterly wind.

We had already broken hands, and once the candles had been lit, the meditation commenced. We sat as individuals but concentrated collectively on the positive energies that were supposedly being created by us.

I have to confess to having felt a trifle conspicuous at this stage, gathered in a circle with candles burning in front of me and holding pieces of amethyst and quartz crystals for good measure. I had begun to wonder, What if some concerned soul mistakenly concluded that we were witches, or even black magicians engaged in a trial ritual run before Samhain the following weekend, and immediately called the police? Or worse still, the local fundamentalist evangelical church, who would doubtless have sent along their disciples to exorcise and purify us! Fortunately, there was no one else in the vicinity, and as our levels of concentration increased so I became acutely aware of atmospheric conditions and changes that were occurring in the setting; whether or not we were being watched seemed irrelevant.

Suddenly three big gusts of wind blew across us. The whole area had begun to feel unsound, and this created an air of foreboding. I interrupted my own concentration in order to scan the surroundings. Everyone sat entirely motionless. There was still no one else about. It was just us—the elements and whatever imbalances in the natural energy currents of Chanctonbury that the group felt needed sorting out.

Both Anne and Amanda had talked about feeling uncomfortable during the Highdown meditation. Now I knew what they meant. I felt it too up at Chanctonbury. As the atmosphere grew more intense the wind quickly gusted again; miraculously the candles that Anne had taken the trouble to light some minutes before somehow managed to avoid being extinguished by the abrupt blast.

However, the setting had begun to be somewhat reminiscent of a scene in the Hammer film version of *The Devil Rides Out*. Only in the film a small group of people created a circle of protection in order to stop demonic forces from coming into their circle; for their pains they were confronted by gusting winds, huge spiders and finally the Angel of Death.

Our little group was attempting to draw negative energies *out* from the surrounding area before exorcizing them and thus restoring the energy balance at the site. I was not expecting any visitations from specifically manifested entities. Even so, this was no film set—it was for real. Everyone remained seated and carried on concentrating. No one uttered a word.

Finally, after fifteen rather fraught minutes had passed, Anne, who assumed the mantle of group leader, asked us all to link hands once more and focus on the energy that had been created on this day to be used for a positive purpose only and for the highest good of all concerned.

She then read the Great Invokation. This supposed to be a particularly potent form of prayer when used by a dedicated group of people applying a visualization technique that involves creating a 'triangle of lighted relationship'—in other words, a form of pyramid power for the good. This

would then link to the highest vibration connected with healing and earth energies—Christ energy. In theory, you couldn't get much higher. Our final exercise was to project the positive energy into the centre of the Ring, letting in the light, and then spread all of it out to the surrounding earth.

One last strong gust of wind soon gave way to a burst of sunlight, which fittingly heralded the end of the high noon deliverance of Chanctonbury Ring. All that remained now was for us to bury the amethyst and rose quartz crystals, which would apparently seal the site with positive energies.

The afternoon's work completed, we headed on down the steep track that led to the bottom of the hill and the carpark feeling a little drained of energy, perhaps because of the intensity of the meditation or the climb to the hill's summit or both. The next stop would be the Black Rabbit public house in Arundel for a well-earned drink and doubtless some after-session analysis as to individual interpretations of our experience at the Ring.

The Rise and Return of Fenris

In the picturesque setting of the Downs and riverbank reeds of the nearby Arun, we sat in the pub garden, and once they had relaxed, the other group members were able to recount their own version of events—which all turned out to be remarkably similar.

Anne had felt there was a dark form emanating from the north side of the Ring, close to where we had previously been seated. Two other members of the group had felt that the negativity was in the earth itself and that it was coming out of the ground. Negativity had to come out of the earth in order to be healed, they maintained.

Amanda probably had the most terrifying experience of anyone present at the meditation. She too was aware that a dark force was below ground, only she had been able to psychically see it as a huge demonic rat-head or black rodent with its jaws open, bearing teeth. It had burst through from the ground below and risen up inside our circle at the Ring, next to her feet. Amanda was absolutely petrified at the sight of this fearsome intruder. Fortunately, she was able to hold the strength of our circle and the light visualization together, and after several attempts at exorcism, the awesome manifestation began to fade in its spectral intensity before finally returning to the earth.

This had occurred shortly after the meditation had begun, simultaneously with the first of the surges of wind that we had experienced. About half way through the healing forum Amanda, along with two other members of the group, had also become aware of another opposing energy force that derived from the centre of the Ring. This was the area where, unbeknown to them, much of the paranormal phenomena recorded at the Ring had occurred, and where Charles Walker had discovered a black altar marked out in stone, containing black candle wax and parchments.

For their part, the healing group had returned from the Ring reassured that their experience and input on the day had resulted in providing a powerful and positive contribution in redressing the energy balance.

But with the very best of intentions at heart, could the effects of centuries of corrupt occult practices at Chanctonbury Ring be negated by a single fifteen-minute spiritual healing session, followed by the customary planting of crystals? And would this possibly deter a supposed black-magic order from carrying out their own foul rites at the Ring during the following weekend's Hallowe'en celebrations? I doubted it.

Still, Chanctonbury had seemed like the right place to start, in view of its history. It would probably require more visitations of a similar nature by the healing group if any long-lasting result was going to be achieved. An important process had begun, and there were other 'gateways' to be visited and cleansed before the earth could go forward towards the New Age and the turn of the millennium, they believed. Only the passing of time would tell if they had been successful or not.

Back at Amanda's place, some three weeks further on, we were discussing those very points. I had been invited there to give an informal talk to the group and some other guests on *The Demonic Connection* and how it linked with the Black Alchemist affair, since no one who was present that evening had read either book. Fittingly enough it was on the night of November 16— which was yet another festival date dedicated to Hekate. Once again it appeared to be the right time to give a small lecture on how aspects of the goddess had figured in and been utilized and corrupted by the likes of the Friends of Hekate and the Black Alchemist for their own purposes.

I had taken along a copy of Andrew Collins's new book *The Second Coming*, which had recently been published. Amanda was thumbing through my copy when she suddenly exclaimed, 'That's it! That's what I saw at the Ring!' She shuddered. I leaned over from my seat and saw what she was pointing at. It was an illustration from Andrew's book, showing the head of the Norse demon-wolf, Fenris, emerging from the interior of the earth, having broken free of its bonds in the underworld. I looked at the illustration once more myself. I could clearly see how Amanda had mistaken the wolf's head for a rat—the head appears rodent-like, with smooth skin and smallish ears. What was particularly intriguing, though, is that Amanda had absolutely no knowledge whatsoever of the illustration's existence, nor of its symbolic meaning, until she saw it in my copy of Andrew's book on that November night.

Other members of the group had also been aware of a 'force beneath the ground' that needed to be nullified and then cleansed. This aspect also fitted the Fenris description and symbolism. None of the group had read any of Andrew's books, either.

During the months that followed the group fragmented, with some of the spiritual healers going their own way and continuing their site cleansing quest, more in smaller groups or individuals than before.

But was there any more information that could be gleaned as to the exact nature and properties of the energies we had been dealing with?

Chapter 12
Ritual Omens

New Veins of Energy

Many writers and researchers of earth energies and the occult are now aware of the natural energies that have flowed both across and beneath the earth's surface for thousands of years. Some believe that there are also in existence new forms of energy, which have not, at present, been registered with scientific instrumentation. These energies are only apparently detectable, at the moment, through their subtle vibrations and echoes, but they are all involved with the whole concept of earth energies at ancient sites.

Andrew Collins had recently carried out extensive research into the so-called orgone energy, first discovered by the Austrian Wilhelm Reich in 1939. Reich had become aware that decaying food and other organic matter discharged luminous blue-green globules only discernable under extreme magnification, which he identified as pulsating forms of energy derived from a biological source. He referred to these energy forms as 'bions', which, when isolated scientifically in metal-linked containers, produced strange side-effects akin to radioactivity.

Reich believed that orgone was universally present in varying degrees and concentrations, both on the ground, in the atmosphere and out in space. A mass-free energy form that flowed from lower concentrations to higher concentrations across the earth, orgone bio forms were attracted to orgone reservoirs, which were either natural or man-enhanced. These orgone 'accumulators' were attracted to 'primary nodal points as sites of discharge', according to Andrew Collins and his investigative team.

They also believed that 'orgone energy discharged by stone circles was projected over the ground to other specifically placed monuments laid out in alignment'. In other words, so-called ley power and orgone energy were virtually one and the same thing.

They were also of the opinion that 'all forms of terrestrial-produced light may be seen as manifestations of orgone deposits located upon the earth's surface'. These light forms included earth lights, shining spheres and some UFOs, which were now being seen as 'luminosities' rather than extra-terrestrial spacecraft.

In his books, ley-line expert Paul Devereux has inferred that some examples of earth lights often appear to possess minds of their own and respond to human thought—thus hinting that this as yet unknown energy form is possibly psycho-interactive. This notion is shared by Andrew Collins, who believes that the human mind can interact with these energy forms and affect them, but it is an extremely subtle vibration that is involved in the process.

Paul Devereux has also associated the earth-lights phenomenon with mountains or hilltop sites. These may take the form of discharges brought about by the stresses of geophysical features, underground tunnels or other land disturbances in association with a varied assortment of atmospheric conditions. In this respect the Clapham site immediately springs to mind, with its church situated as it is on a hilltop site beneath which are ground disturbances. Many 'luminosities' have been seen here, of course, along with other paranormal phenomena spanning a period of three decades.

But if we are now able to define the so-called ley power as orgone, and if the human mind can possibly interact with and influence this power, then other people will also be aware of its potential and will have drawn the same conclusion. It seems likely, too, that the likes of the Friends of Hekate were onto it some time ago, and if indeed this is the case it would certainly account for much of the unexplained paranormal phenomena at such sites as Clapham, Chanctonbury and others.

Reich was probably the first scientist of his kind to be able actually to establish that a real magical force could be produced and quantified in the laboratory. He carried out his experiments into orgone energy at the institute named after him in Rangeley, Maine, on the north-eastern coast of the USA, close to the border with Canada. But in 1951 his work took a turn for the worse, and had a devastating effect on the area. Reich had been experimenting with orgone energy and electromagnetism using atomic radiation as a medium. The Oranur experiment, as it was known, helped to create a monster—not literally, but in the form of DOR (deadly orgone radiation), a life-threatening element in direct opposition to OR (orgone radiation).

Strange things started to happen in and around the institute. Employees and visitors alike became ill; objects would suddenly disappear, and then, just as bafflingly, reappear. Unexplained lights were seen in the vicinity of

the institute, and Reich himself was believed to have seen UFOs in the woods close to Rangeley.

The atmosphere around Rangeley became contaminated; trees and other foliage began to twist and wither: the landscape itself felt as if an overbearing presence had drained it of its natural attributes. The DOR was being fed by the natural orgone energy, and there seemed to be no way of reversing the process.

Reich left Rangeley and headed for Tucson, Arizona, where he set up a new but smaller institute. Here he directed atmospheric and weather-control experiments in an attempt to negate the DOR effects that had so devastated the project at Rangeley.

In fact, the experiments in Tucson turned out to be far more successful than they had been in Maine. But US government agencies and departments had been causing Reich trouble for some years, and this soon escalated into a policy aimed at destroying Reich's reputation together with his life's work. In 1954 he was ordered by the US Food and Drug Administration, through the courts, to stop all orgone research and cease publication of material on the subject. They also banned Reich's ten most prominent books, while other book stocks containing his works and unpublished papers were destroyed. They went after everything of Reich's that they could get their hands on. Proposed transportation of orgone accumulators was suspended, and any still in circulation were located and taken apart; other relevant laboratory apparatus was confiscated.

Further legal action by the US authorities followed, resulting in Reich being charged with contempt of court and subsequently jailed. He died a broken man, in a federal penitentiary, in 1957. The whole affair reeked of a cover-up.

I began to wonder. If DOR had drained the natural orgone energy of its positive properties in Rangeley, thus contaminating the local climate, and considering the possibility that the human mind, when focused accordingly, can link with and affect such energies, could a similar type of process occur if a group of corrupt occultists had tried to psychically interact with and influence natural orgone power, or similar types of energies, for their own negative purposes?

Would this be akin to drawing from the positive and thus creating a negative or malign atmospheric situation at the particular locations that were being used in this respect? If so, could this possibly have accounted for the similar conditions experienced at Clapham and Chanctonbury?

Andrew Collins had researched into orgone mainly in connection with energies that were possibly behind the crop-circle phenomenon, publishing

his findings in his self-published book, *The Circle Makers*. Yet orgone seemed also to lie at the core of the arcane energies at ancient sites theory. Crop circles had appeared along the section of the A259 road known as 'Long Furlong', which links the Clapham and Chanctonbury sites.

There had been reported finds of crop circles in the vicinity of Avebury, too—a location that had been mentioned in connection with the Friends of Hekate. I decided to take a closer look at the configuration of Avebury, Silbury and the West Kennett Long Barrow.

Through their shape, the long barrows—particularly West Kennett—are representative of the death goddess, whose time begins at Samhain and extends towards winter. She is known in Britain as Cailleach , and her sacred talisman is variously the Moon, sickle or scissors (like Hekate), which is carried by the last of the three Fates, or Norns. Cailleach guards the entrance to the 'dark cycle' of the year; she is also linked to Kali, as both are destroyers, or black goddesses, and Kali is also depicted brandishing knives—cutting instruments.

Silbury Hill was also linked to goddess worship, so this was a place that needed further investigation, particularly as it was situated so close to the West Kennett Long Barrow.

Hill of the Winter Goddess

The earliest phase of Silbury Hill, situated almost due south of Avebury, was erected just over 4000 years ago, and it seems to have been enlarged at three or four different points in history, culminating in its completion *c.* 2780 BC, in the late Neolithic period.

Renowned as the greatest artificial mound in Europe, Silbury Hill stands close to the Stone Age cathedral at Avebury. The hill's precise purpose has always baffled archaeologists, who have never been able to prove whether it was a tomb especially built for a prehistoric chieftain. Inevitable tales of vast treasures buried beneath it have only added to the aura of mystery.

It was largely to discover whether there was any truth in these stories that the earliest attempts to dig into the mound were made in 1776 (with a vertical shaft) and 1849 (with a horizontal shaft). A more modern archaeological excavation was undertaken between 1967 and 1970. These findings showed that the mound was built along very similar lines of inner-platform construction as had been used by the Ancient Egyptians in building the pyramids.

Author John Michell (*The View Over Atlantis*, 1973) had deduced that judging by its circular flattened top, Silbury Hill 'was evidently a place for sacrifice' as opposed to a burial ground.

Moses B. Cotsworth, a scholar from York who had concluded that many of the great ancient monuments were constructed in correlation with astronomy, estimated that a large pole, ninety-five feet in height, once stood on top of Silbury Hill, casting a shadow onto the deliberately flattened land to the north. He was further convinced that a fixing marker would be found at the precise point where the shadow was cast by the midday sun on the winter solstice—a theory that was proved to be correct, as there was indeed a small but accurately placed boulder engraved with strange symbols, including that of a fish.

In his book *The Silbury Treasure* (1976) Michael Dames referred to Silbury Hill as representing the winter goddess. The mound stands 130 feet high and measures 100 feet across the top, and took an estimated eighteen million man-hours to construct. Legend has it that Silbury was accidentally created by the Devil, who was building Wansdyke when he was compelled by the priests of Avebury Circle to wipe his spade and empty the resulting sack of earth, which formed Silbury Hill.

A pyschometrist, Olive Pixley, visited the hill with writer John Foster Forbes, and they felt that the mound was created in order to cover up a previous stone circle that had stood on the site thousands of years ago. Black-magic rites had occurred there, which had led to a build up of negative energies resulting in an ambience of evil that was so profound that in order to neutralize it the circle had been destroyed and the stones buried.

Some evidence went part of the way to backing up this theory when stones were discovered during one of the early excavations in 1849. Later, in 1969, some boulders and small stones similar to the one found by Moses B. Cotsworth, but without symbols, were also uncovered.

The Primordial Powerhouse

The Avebury Ring, which is even older than Stonehenge, had also been referred to as a 'Stone Age powerhouse' by some occult writers. The antiquarian Dr Williams Stukely had studied the stones for over thirty years during the early part of the 18th Century. He was able to identify the stone avenues, which extended from the main circle, as forming the pattern of the 'solar serpent'.

Most of these stones were destroyed during Stukely's time, however, only two remaining today; so effective was their eradication that there is no reference to them in the Avebury guidebook. One remaining clue to the existence of the serpent avenue of stones lies in the area that was once the serpent's head, originally formed by a double circle of stones, which lies on the southern point of Hackpen Hill. The name 'hac pen' means serpent's head.

Both the Avebury Ring and Silbury Hill have been named in connection

with the activities of the Friends of Hekate, but at present there is no real evidence to substantiate any ritualistic pursuits, unlike that which Charles discovered in the nearby West Kennett Long Barrow.

It is worth noting that the Avebury ring, Silbury Hill and the West Kennett Long Barrow are all within a few minutes' walking distance from each other. There is a linear configuration here, as the West Kennett Long Barrow is at the base of an alignment that cuts through one side of Silbury Hill and right through Avebury. Using the West Kennett Long Barrow as a pivotal axis, there is another alignment running through the centre of Silbury Hill and Windmill Hill. To the west of Avebury is the site of Oldbury, where there is a white horse carved into the hillside. According to John Michell one of the country's most lengthy ley lines runs through the southern perimeter of the Avebury ring. It runs from Bury St Edmunds, Suffolk, and travels through several churches dedicated to St Michael, including Glastonbury Tor, before petering out at Land's End, Cornwall.

The Blackened Tomb

August 29, 1994. As we pulled into the car park just beyond Silbury Hill, which was situated slightly to the right of us, I was reminded once again that this, the largest man-made mound in Europe, was constructed of alternating layers of organic and inorganic material, which make it an ideal accumulator of organic energy along with other tumuli and barrows as primary 'nodal points'.

Silbury Hill lies to the north-west of the West Kennett Long Barrow, and it was to the latter that we made our way first to see what, if any, recent occult activities had taken place. As we trudged up the narrow track that leads to the complex I became aware of a feeling of isolation—a not uncommon experience, despite being in close proximity to the main road.

Charles had made several significant finds at the West Kennett Long Barrow during the past decade or so. The first of these was on August 2, 1985 during his first visit to the tomb where, acting on Elymas's information that the site was probably being used by a group practising forms of corrupt magical rites, Charles found a rather complex magical symbol inscribed in black on the north-west chamber ceiling.

The symbol took the form of a horizontal bar measuring ten inches in length, with additional graphics that twisted around it. This was bisected by an unusual vertical or crosspiece of slightly longer length (twelve inches) containing similar graphics save for the top end, which formed an upright rectangle. It was similar to those symbols used in the grimoires of Solomon, particularly the *Lemegeton*.

This text, also known as the *Lesser Key of Solomon the King*, is a work of pure

demonic magic, regarded as one of the definitive grimoires by 17th-century occultists. It contains seventy-two seals, and having checked all of them and other sigils too, notably in the *Book of Black Magic* by A. E. Waite, I could find nothing, at present, that replicates the West Kennett seal. Moreover, this appeared, in part, to be a combination of several seals, making it a hybrid and peculiar to the group.

Elymas himself went to the West Kennett site, together with two of his leading coven members, shortly after November 1, 1989, and immediately on entering the tomb complex found the atmosphere to be 'very heavy'. A strong negative force had been raised for a specific and important purpose, they felt. 'Whoever was responsible had a very good reason—in their mind at least—for doing the ritual, and had really put their whole self, body and mind, into it,' Elymas said afterwards.

He also stated that it must have been 'catastrophic' for whoever the ritual was directed towards. If it wasn't an individual then the resulting influence that their actions had over a particular section or some event was tremendous.

In fact, Elymas and both his colleagues had felt utterly drained of the natural life-force energies on emerging from the tomb. The atmosphere had been so bad while they were in there that they felt unable to stay too long. It took them a while to recover.

Earlier on that year, Helen, the South London psychic, had described—without actually naming it—an ancient tomb complex to Andrew, which he had identified as the West Kennett Long Barrow; Helen had psychically seen members of the reformed Friends of Hekate/Dark Council conducting a corrupt magical ritual.

Helen had no knowledge whatsoever of the West Kennet site's history or of Charles's recent investigations into it. Was it possible, therefore, that Elymas and his two associates had stumbled on the aftermath of a Dark Council rite? It would certainly be some time before they ever went near that particular site again.

Two years on—on July 21, 1991—Charles found a section of animal jawbone which had been deliberately placed on a ledge in the centre of the west chamber, well above eye level. I took this to the Hove Natural History Museum, where further analysis revealed that it was in fact part of the jawbone of a nine-month-old goat or lamb that had probably been ritually sacrificed. Around the jawbone were the remains of black candle wax, which had been burnt into the wall of the tomb, giving it a dark and sinister look; there was also musk incense, which had been arranged with the wax in a circle, with the jawbone forming the head or altar.

A number of other items were also found in the large west chamber. Various remains of red and white candles, plus more wax, which had, once again, been burnt into the stone. There were also the remains of a beeswax close to the jawbone. A quartz crystal pendant with a silver cross-piece top had been placed a little further to the right of the beeswax.

Returning to the West Kennet site a little later that year on August 24, Charles had found a near perfect pentagram—not inverted—surrounded by two circles, and drawn in white chalk at the tomb entrance on the east side of the complex. Inside the large west chamber part of the magical talisman for the planet Saturn had been inscribed on the chamber wall.

The main areas where occult symbols and artefacts had been found together with the remnants of rituals were in the west and north chambers, in precise opposition to the east, the Christian altar.

In ancient times, our ancestors would partake in various rituals which in all probability were conducted at a separate location close by before taking the remnants of funeral feasts and ritual offerings to the chambered tombs and scattering them afterwards.

Was this aspect of the Old Worship being reinstated by the individuals who were responsible for some of the artefacts that had been discovered at West Kennett? Not all of these had been planted by the same group, either, it seemed.

I decided to ask a fully qualified practising healer to sense the energy types of the artefacts—with quite interesting results, which confirmed my own theories. The section of goat's or sheep's jawbone was completely 'dead', thus intimating that its life force may well have been appropriated by some kind of ritual sacrifice. The red and white candles were still emitting negative energies, so the healer had felt the need to conduct a form of protection ritual in order to combat these and any detrimental effects that may have resulted.

However, the beeswax was positive and the glass crystal pendant was hot with similar energies. This was quite an unusual item, measuring little more than an inch in length. The crosspiece was constructed out of three silver rings, two of which were attached on either side to a silver top, which held the crystal. The crystal itself was half an inch long, made out of quartz and tapering to a blunted point. The (clear) quartz crystal is known to activate all level of consciousness by giving full spectrum energy. According to the 'Crystal Awareness Guide' (a pamphlet), it dispels negativity in one's energy field and environment.

It also receives, stores, activates, amplifies and transmits energy, while being excellent for meditation. In other words, its function at West Kennett was to counteract the immense build-up of negative forces. In theory it

shouldn't have been removed from its resting place, a state of affairs that has now been rectified by replacing it with another crystal.

It seemed that we had reached a situation whereby some 'New Age' pagan or possibly healing group had twigged that the West Kennett Long Barrow was being worked by a group of corrupt occultists and had tried to cleanse and nullify the negative elements by placing protective charms at the site.

The Runic Warning

On July 5 1992, Charles made one of his most significant discoveries at the Long Barrow. On entering the tomb complex he noticed immediately that the smell of incense was more powerful than on previous occasions, to the point of being almost overwhelming. Charles made his way towards the west chamber together with his camcorder video camera. If there was any further evidence of corrupt occult practices it could be recorded on video, and the west chamber remained the most likely place where any such evidence would be found.

Carefully scrutinizing the west chamber wall of the blackened tomb, he could easily make out three rows of runic symbols, each one placed below the next, all in line and chalked in white. An inverted pentagram, also in white chalk, was positioned next to, and to the right of, the runic symbols.

The word 'rune' is derived from the German word *Raunen*, which apparently had a dual meaning. One transcription declares that *Raunen* comes from the ancient Low German, which means to carve, or cut. Hence during the early times the runes were carved, not written. However, another interpretation of *Raunen* specifies that it originates from Old Norse and means 'mystery or secret'.

Runes were first used for magical rituals by the ancient races and only later were they appropriated as a form of writing. They were held to be secret throughout the Anglo-Saxon communities—where the word 'rune' was common to both the old Anglo-Saxon and Icelandic language, and is said to relate to forms of magic. The exact origin of runes, though, remains

Fig 5 The runic message plus inverted pentagram also found at West Kennett—but what was its purpose?

somewhat of a mystery, some believing that they are non-Teutonic in ancestry, probably stemming from Ancient Greece or Phoenicia. Runes were used for divination, and were considered to be extremely potent symbols. They have been discovered inscribed on ancient stone monuments and other artefacts all over Europe.

There are various interpretations of the runes. The earliest version, the 'old Teutonic runes' consisted of twenty-four letters arranged in three rows of eight. Later on the Anglo-Saxons added a further nine. The twenty-four original runes were said to be magical, and each column of eight was separately dedicated to a Norse deity. These in turn were known as Freya's Eight, Hagal's Eight and Tiw's Eight. However, they were venerable to Odin—Lord of the Runes and patron of all magic.

Runes have also been segregated into three separate systems—English, German and Scandinavian, but any distinction between them is purely parochial. The significance of a sacred triad is apparent in all the age-old ideologies, from ancient druidism to the Egyptians.

The three sets of runes that were discovered by Charles at the West Kennett Long Barrow were a mixture of Germanic and Norse runic glyphs, and they proved a little awkward to translate.

I had, however, been able to purchase some invaluable books on the subject, which had enabled me to provide a reasonably in-depth definition. The bottom line, I learned, refers to the future invocation of a spirit or entity. The top line, when read in an alphabetical sense, translates to the word 'rowan'. The rowan tree or mountain ash was believed to have had a significant role in the rituals of the druids. Sanctified fires, particularly those used in the rites of Beltane and Samhain, were made from rowan wood. It was essential for either rowan, oak or yew wood to be burnt for the really important rituals. Rowans were trees of protection, and they were frequently discovered near stone circles. The rowan was believed to provide protection against witchcraft and the evil eye. Its symbolism was steeped in old folklore, particularly in Scotland and the Highlands. The goddess of the rowan tree is Rowana or Rauni. She is the patroness of the arcane wisdom of the runes, and her festival date is July 15—ten days after Charles had discovered the runic glyphs.

However, there appeared to be no literal alphabetical translation for the middle line of symbols discovered at West Kennett. This line, positioned next to the inverted pentagram, would seem to fall into the category of symbolic rather than alphabetical runes. Four of the six runes in this line come from Hagl's Aett and are Germanic in origin (meaning 'Hagal's Eight'). The 'Hagalaz' or H rune, the second glyph in the middle row, is said to hold 'The mystery of the framework of the world and defines the primal form of the multiverse', according to Edred Thorsson in his handbook of rune magic entitled *Futhark* (1994).

The author also describes Hagalaz as 'the complete model containing the potential energy of neutral power in the multiverse, which is born from the dynamic, generating, evolving unity of fire (energy and ice antimatter).

In its capacity within the elements, the Hagal rune is also known as the rune of air. A gentle breeze can immediately be whipped up into a storm, and this related to the force of the Wyrd, which flows like the wind. Hagal is also the hailstone, and in the old Anglo-Saxon rune verse it denotes the strength and influence of the Wyrd to govern the destiny of the human race.

In The *Wisdom of the Runes* (1985) Michael Howard says: 'The victims of the Wyrd's capricious influence may feel they are being swept along by forces which they cannot control'. The power of the Wyrd is not something that can be controlled by man alone. In this respect it is more a question of going with the flow and working with the Wyrd rather than trying to combat it.

Wyrd was a name that Debbie had picked up in connection with the activities of the People of Hexe. Six-legged spiders were symbols that had been deliberately placed beneath the ground, some as earth-energy blockage markers, by the People of Hexe in order for them to redefine the energy patterns. The effect resulting from this—their own interaction with the energy matrix—correlated directly with the Web of Wyrd, the symbolism of which was at the heart of their ambitions.

Quite the most significant find associated with the People of Hexe occurred on November 2, 1991 at Whitby Abbey in Yorkshire, where Andrew Collins's team unearthed an antique silver-plated trident fork covered on both sides with runic symbols. The inscriptions on the fork were from Germanic rune lore, and after careful analysis Andrew concluded that whoever had inscribed them possessed a proficient knowledge of Germanic runes.

They were similar to the ones that Charles was to discover on the west chamber wall at the long barrow, only there was no question here of copycat symbols being used at West Kennett, because Andrew's findings were not published until 1993—one year after Charles had discovered the chalk inscriptions at the West Kennet tomb.

Some of the Germanic runes were common to both sets of glyphs, notably the Hagalaz, and H also relates to the number eight, being that it is the eighth letter of the alphabet. Hagal can be a disruptive force but also a protective sigil; however, as Andrew Collins readily points out in *The Second Coming*, Hagal is also the magical name of the Romanian rune-master who had apparently transferred the Fenris wolf to Britain.

Among the other runes from the middle row found at West Kennett was the N rune, which, in one of its facets, symbolizes the idea of coming into manifestation; but it is also seen as a strong rune of protection. The other rune of significance was the Eolh or Elhaz—another symbol of protection and, according to Michael Howard, 'a secret sign used for recognition purposes by followers of the medieval witch cult who were traditionally worshippers of the pagan Horned God'.

Whoever had inscribed the three rows of runic symbols on the west chamber wall at the West Kennett tomb complex obviously possessed a fairly comprehensive knowledge of runic symbols.

The references to rowan and the other runes symbolizing power and protection signifies that their purpose may have been to counteract yet more forthcoming negativity set to be produced by corrupt occultists. The inverted pentagram could have been drawn next to the symbols to emphasize precisely that point.

The alternative was, of course, that the unscrupulous occultists themselves were responsible for chalking up the glyphs, which was probably their way of saying that the power of the runes was now in their hands—or so they believed.

Charles had discovered the runic symbols on July 5, 1992, just two days after the beginning of the 'Dog Days' in pagan lore. This period, ruled by the Dog Star, Sirius, is called 'Loki's Brand' in the northern tradition. Loki's offspring can be interpreted in Norse as the great beast, one of the forms of the Antichrist (see Chapter 9). The inverted pentagram deliberately inscribed next to the runes could also be seen as a symbol used by the group responsible to raise some sort of Antichrist entity.

Either way, the runic symbol, together with the pentagram of Kali Yuga, had the word 'warning' secretly written all over it.

Guardians of the Shades?

As we reached the entrance to the tomb after completing the steady climb up the narrow track, I couldn't help wondering what, if anything, we would find inside this time.

On first entering the entombed passage we were immediately aware of a thick, potent smell of incense. This was nothing new, but as we made our way towards the west chamber, we could just make out human figures and realized that something was currently being burned inside there.

As we entered, the two figures we had caught sight of—a man and a woman—were both seated, one either side of the entrance, slumped against the stone wall of the west chamber interior, with their legs outstretched

partially across the entrance itself. Both were bare-foot and aged approximately in their early twenties.

The young woman had short dark hair and was slim. The young man had dark, unkempt shoulder-length hair and a fringe, which covered his eyebrows and revealed rather staring eyes. He had a somewhat bulbous nose, small moustache and wispy beard. He was accompanied by a young dog, which, when we first entered, he spent a lot of time petting and calming. He also had a reporter's notebook and pen in his hands, but he was not writing anything.

A candle and some incense were burning in one of the alcoves immediately above where the female was sitting. From the atmosphere inside the tomb, which was heavy with the build-up of incense, it seemed that they had been there for some time, probably all day or longer, and judging by their positions, they didn't look as though they were about to move—not for anyone—despite the lack of space in the claustrophobic chamber.

They appeared not to respond in any way to our presence: they did not speak a single word or attempt to engage in any eye contact, not even to acknowledge each other while we were there, yet we were aware that they were indeed being attentive to our conversation which I and my two associates deliberately kept on a routine level.

Neither of the two people seated in the chamber seemed at all friendly—quite the reverse. The general atmosphere they created by being there in the manner that they were made everyone who entered the chamber feel uncomfortable and unwelcome. If this was a deliberate strategy on their part, it certainly worked. What, we wondered, were they doing in there?

Outside it was a warm, sunny August day with clear, refreshing air—perfect conditions for being outside, so there was no need for them to be inside, surely, with an active young dog straining at the leash. I had been about to tentatively attempt some form of open conversation with them when some other people came in, followed by a troupe of beefy-looking German motorcyclists, and the situation inside the chamber became rather chaotic, as, despite these further new arrivals, the immovable pair still refused to budge from their seated positions inside the west chamber.

With the overcrowded conditions we decided to move back to the entrance of the whole tomb complex, where we stayed for a while.

I gazed up at the standing sarsens that form the construction of this chambered long barrow. These large stones are extremely ancient, dating back some seventy million years, whereas the tomb itself is a mere 5000 years old. Contained in the complex are two pairs of burial chambers, one pair on each side. Access is via the central entrance, which I was standing under, and which in turn leads to the west chamber at the end, thus making five in all.

In normal circumstances people visiting the West Kennett Long Barrow spend at least ten to fifteen minutes looking around the inside before leaving. However, on this occasion it was noticeable that most of the sightseers who came in were out again very quickly—even the German bikers had come out within a few minutes, looking slightly bemused, and they were obviously people who were not used to being prevented in any way from what they wanted to do.

The situation within the entombed complex had developed into something fairly bizarre. So exactly who were these on-site guardians who were resident in the west chamber, and what was their precise purpose in remaining there?

It was possible, of course, that they had no connection whatsoever with the occult and just happened to be sitting inside the long barrow by coincidence. Perhaps they were part of the pagan group who had tried to clean up the site and were keeping an eye out for any untoward occultists that might turn up. However, their demeanour and behaviour seemed to be at odds with these notions, which left us with the distinct probability that they had been installed in the west chamber as guardians and/or to prepare the site for a forthcoming meeting or something important. But the big questions were, what exactly? And for whom?

Chapter 13

Spinners of fate

Sigils and Spirals

'If I were a black magician, I wouldn't use West Kennett', Andrew Collins told me when I had discussed the West Kennett situation with him. Andrew is not a magician of any sort, black or otherwise, but watching the steady trickle of people come and go from this ancient burial site I could see what he meant. Being that it is situated in such close proximity to Silbury Hill and the Avebury Ring, West Kennett does get its share of visitors, but most tend to by-pass it in favour of the other two more famous landmarks. Very few people, if any, are likely to be drawn up to the long barrow after dusk, as Charles can testify, having made several visits there at night himself.

One of his earliest discoveries there on August 2, 1985, besides the magical symbol on the north-west chamber ceiling, was at the entrance to the west chamber itself. Just below each of the ledges at the entrance, a series of hexagrams (six-pointed stars) had been drawn, one on top of another and out of alignment, thereby giving a multi-image effect. They were constructed by drawing two interacting triangles, one inverted in a similar manner to the Seal of Solomon, only less perfect.

The hexagrams were apparently being used as a form of magical protection for the particular groups working the site: their intention was to provide a deterrent to anyone attempting to interfere.

Hexagrams, segments of animal bone and quartz crystal, together with the combination of Germanic and Norse runic symbols that had been found inside the west chamber, were all familiar to Andrew Collins in relation to artefacts that had been deliberately planted at other ancient sites by the People of Hexe.

Yet, as he was quick to point out, the objects that his team had been able to retrieve in those instances had all been secreted beneath the ground, or in

some out-of-the-way place, unlike the runic glyphs that had been inscribed on the west chamber wall; the work of the People of Hexe was not on view for others to discover.

But the fact still remained that some of the occult calling cards that had been inscribed in the tomb complex were similar to those used by the Hexe group. Some of the symbols had first appeared at West Kennett as long ago as 1985, whereas Andrew's book, *The Second Coming*, which chronicles the artefacts and symbols used by the People of Hexe, was not published until the summer of 1993.

During 1991, Elymas had been told by one his sources that an occult group had been using the West Kennett site as a meeting place for new recruits. They had not actually performed any rituals at the site, according to the source, but had held a type of celebration during which they had admitted a number of new members to their group.

It was not unreasonable to assume that any rituals of significance had been carried out elsewhere along the energy configuration, with some sort of seating ceremony occurring at the tomb. Elymas had no doubts, in view of his own experiences at West Kennett, that the tomb was used by what he referred to as 'serious occultists' who were involved in the much 'darker side' of the occult.

It was quite conceivable that the Dark Council had used the West Kennett Long Barrow on an occasional basis before moving on elsewhere, leaving the fringe of outer circle members to appropriate it ; it could be that they were the ones leaving a certain amount of evidence behind—something that the central hierarchy would never do.

In this respect, had the area been used as some kind of 'proving ground' for new members, in a similar manner to that described by Mary in relation to the methods allegedly adopted by the Friends of Hekate during the mid-1970s at Clapham, Chanctonbury Ring and supposedly nearby Avebury, too?

During our time in the west chamber at the West Kennet complex, I'd been able to scrutinize it for any further clues in the manner of occult seals inscribed on the wall, while all the time being under the watchful eyes of the site guardians.

However, the west chamber had been cleaned up, only the faded remains of what appeared to be the runic symbols were still visible. There was nothing new in the west chamber. In the south-eastern chamber, though, three circular maze or spiral patterns had recently been inscribed in white chalk on the chamber wall, two being positioned side by side with the third, slightly smaller one, underneath. They were formed by five graded circles measuring approximately six inches in diameter, with a link-thread running from right to left and then underneath.

Three runic glyphs had been drawn, strategically placed outside the three coiled patterns. The symbol placed outside the left-hand circle was the same as one of the glyphs that had been chalked in the middle row of three sets that had appeared on the west chamber wall next to the pentagram of Kali Yuga. It was the Elhaz rune, which besides being a symbol of protection was also used as a secret sign of recognition by devotees of the witch cult.

Underneath the lower spiral pattern the 'Ing' rune had been chalked in white in its variant Anglo-Saxon form. This rune derives from Ingwaz, who was said to have been an old Germanic earth god who represented the male consort of the earth-mother goddess of fertility and nurture known as Nerthus. The Ing-Nerthus cult emphasizes the feminine aspect, as the female devours the male in order to recharge her powers after they had been sapped by making the land fertile.

This rune also represents gestating energy that must be contained in an incubative form so that its power can increase before it can be manifested and turbulently discharged during a special ritual. It betokens the completion of a particular cycle.

Finally the 'W' rune, placed outside the right-hand spiral and drawn the reverse way round, symbolically relates to the binding together of several different types of power for a desired purpose, and has the planet Saturn as one of its rulers.

It certainly seemed that some potent rune magic was being worked at West Kennett, but by whom and exactly how it was being used was anyone's guess.

What of the three interlinked spiral patterns—what was their significance? Mazes or maze patterns are not uncommon, and there are examples of two interlinked maze patterns inscribed into stone by our ancient ancestors, notably at Newgrange Parsonage grave in County Meath, Ireland.

Maze or spiral patterns inscribed into stone monoliths are believed by some to be prehistoric representations of crop circles and energy lines.

The Dance of the Labyrinth
A good number of spiral shapes are to be found at tomb sites, where spiral etchings can often be seen on the walls. In Ancient Egypt, maze patterns were left on seals in graves, and festivals consisting of ritual dance and the slaying of a bull were performed in a maze complex.

A comparable cult also involves a bull-type creature in the form of the Minotaur or bull of Minos, which resided in a mysterious underground labyrinth in ancient Crete, and which was slain by Prince Theseus.

Being that the Cretan labyrinth was supposed to have been underground,

it became associated with demons from the underworld. According to Geoffrey Ashe the Cretan labyrinth appears to start in the form of a dance. 'A file of dancers performed it on a ritual floor, following the septenary backtracking spiral. Cretan coins reproduce the pattern,' he says in his *Mythology of the British Isles* (1990).

A passage in Virgil's *Aeneid* refers to a ceremonial dance carried out by Trojan youths (*c*. 100 BC) in which the weaving movements were said to be symbolic of the spirals of the Cretan maze. This became a religious ritual of prodigious significance, which took place annually at Rome and was known as the Troia. It was described by scholar Jackson Knight as being 'intended to create a magical field of exclusive force, an abstract defensive entanglement'.

The word 'Troy' is derived from ancient Indo-European and means 'turning'. The Roman Troia may well have taken its name from the coiling dance ritual rather than the more logical association with the ancient city of Troy, as the earliest maze spiral patterns predate the Roman Empire by several millennia, and there was never, apparently, a notable labyrinth at Troy itself.

Ashe postulates that further back both the Trojan and Cretan maze dances could well have been linked to goddess worship. The goddess for whom the labyrinth was created as a form of her own personification is Ariadne, whose symbolism involves using the spiral thread in order to reach the labyrinth's inner core—and whom Robert Graves links to Arianrhod, the goddess of the Silver Wheel (see Chapter 6).

In *Egypt before Herodotus* T. D. Kendrick speculates that the Trojan rituals and worship originated from Samothrace and the veneration of the Cabiri— a race of people described by the first-century Greek historian Strabo as 'ministers of Hekate' (see Chapter 2). The labyrinth dance is said to betoken entry into the 'mysteries of the other world' and Christianity adapted this notion. Spiral or maze patterns can be seen in early churches.

Chartres and St Catherine

Chartres Cathedral in northern France contains a labyrinth-style design which was built into the nave during the cathedral's construction in the late 12th century. The original brass plate from the centre of the Chartres maze has since disappeared, but the occultist Fulcanelli (*Le Mystère des cathédrales*, 1926) noted that early drawings of the original plate showed Theseus and the Minotaur in combat, thus linking it specifically to the ancient Cretan labyrinth. At the centre of the Chartres design is a six-petalled marble flower, which is believed to be a representation of the Seal of Solomon. This particular seal is constructed from two triangles—one upright, the other inverted, and both interacting in order to create the six-rayed star design, which would be consonant with the centre of the Chartres maze.

The centre of the Seal of Solomon is said to symbolize the quintessence, or the so-called fifth element, an abstract but powerful life source which was also equated with the Chartres maze centre. The christianized symbolism of Chartres and the Virgin Mary is in stark contrast to the darkness of the subterranean Cretan labyrinth with its centred demonic figure of the Minotaur. The medieval concept of the earth and the cosmos was often perceived as a maze plan or layered wheel, with grades or circles displaying the zodiac on the outside and descending down to the 'infernus' or hell at the centre.

There is enough evidence to suggest that an earlier maze existed at Chartres, which related to the dark Cretan labyrinth before the christianization of Chartres itself. Several centuries before the construction of the current cathedral the crypt or underground chamber at the Chartres site contained an idol of the mysterious Black Virgin, whose cult had been linked to both Hekate and St Catherine.

In his book *The Cult of the Black Virgin* (*op. cit.*) Ean Begg dates its coming to Chartres as AD 876, when Charles the Bald transferred the *chemise* (casing) of the Virgin from Aachen to Chartres, where the 'Cult of a holy well of the strong and of the Virgin who wilt give birth' was apparently evident.

There are several Black Virgins in this area, including one specifically identified with Hekate. In fact the provinces of Chartres, Champagne and Blois all came under the jurisdiction of the House of Blois in medieval France.

The Count of Blois at this time was Theobald, who was considered to be a 'man of much consequence' in his own country, and a person to whom the Norman barons could instinctively turn. As well as being the Count of Blois, Champagne and Chartres. Theobald was elder brother to King Stephen de Blois and to Henry, Bishop of Winchester, the possible inaugurator of St Catherine's cult in Britain.

In his book *The Second Coming* (*op. cit.*), Andrew Collins tells us that 'The Winchester Miz-Maze is a square, debased version of the so-called Chartres design'. He also believes that in addition to the chapel upon St Catherine's Hill, Winchester, Henry de Blois could well have been responsible for the construction of the original turf-cut Miz-Maze there—which may indeed have been imported from the design of the earlier Chartres maze by such as Henry de Blois.

The exact date of the Winchester turf maze construction, however, remains somewhat of a mystery. In its present form it is thought to be approximately 300 years old, but maze expert Jeff Saward thinks that there was an earlier one at the same location, dating back to the 1200s.

While researching to find any further clues concerning the Winchester

Miz-Maze mystery, I found an intriguing reference to the maze at St Catherine's Hill, Winchester, in a guide book to the countryside and ancient sites, for which one of the researchers was Eric Maple, author of *Supernatural England* (1977). Maple stated that the Winchester turf maze 'may even be of prehistoric origin, possibly connected with a religious dance ritual'. If correct, this means that the Winchester Miz-Maze could be a lot older than previously envisaged, albeit that it took a rougher or more primitive form.

The Mystic Wheel of Hagal

The trio of interlinked spiral patterns accompanied by the runic symbols at West Kennett indicated the arousal and subsequent harnessing of energies by those who were responsible for the inscription.

The day of my West Kennett visit, August 29, marks the start of the Runic half-month of Rad—a period when the correct channelling of energies can produce the required results. August 29 is also the Festival of Urdr, the eldest of the three Norns (Fates). These were, of course, the designators of ultimate fate, spinners who held the threads of destiny in their hands. Urdr and the Norns were known to the Anglo-Saxons as Wyrd—and the Web of Wyrd was at the heart of the People of Hexes' plans for redefining the energy matrix.

The name 'wyrd' is linked to the German *werden*, which means 'to become'. Wyrd is also associated with the Old Germanic words meaning spindle, which are *wirt* and *wirtel*.

In *Runic Astrology* (1995), Nigel Pennick's excellent and in-depth study of runic concepts, cycles and powers, the author explains the complexities of the Wyrd and its symbolic relationship with the cosmos. The Wyrd's imagery in this respect involves the spindle in the sky and the distaff, which are hallowed symbols of the goddess Frigg and the Norns. These symbols are other names for stars that are better known as the trio who go to make up Orion's Belt in the heavens.

The three Norns are also known as the three 'weird sisters'—Urdr, Verdandi and Skuld. Their names mean past, present and future. They are not subservient to any other gods—only to the paramount energy of the universe itself, known as Orlog, the ultimate conductor of the Web of Wyrd.

The rotating spindle is said to represent the universe in this symbolism. The goddess Frigg rules time and the skies. She had spun the thread that is woven by the Norns. In a planetary sense, the 'loom of creation' is also associated with the earth cycles, time scales, and this is emblematic of the labyrinth and in particular the thread symbolically spun by the weavers of time and space.

Urdr—the eldest of the three Norns—is linked to the rune Hagal by

virtue of the fact that both Hagal and Urdr are associated with the past. Hagal denotes the arousal of erstwhile energies to be applied in a current situation, and it is also the rune of Samhain. Hagal's tree is the yew, as is Hekate's. Hagal also had a strong feminine aspect because it is referred to as the 'mother rune', often at the root of all matters.

Hagal is an open door to the nexus between the upper, middle and lower planes. In a tangible sense these access points were physically betokened by such things as crossroads—traditionally a favourite haunt of Hekate's—or sometimes standing stones and similar locations, which could be identified as central to a particular grouping in a landscape.

In the northern tradition, one aspect of the sacred geometrical pattern comprises the Hagal grid, a series of overlapping ornamental hexagonal patterns, which forms the framework for a complete hexagram shape. This symbolism relates to Hagal's icy state as ice crystals, quartz or hailstones forming crystalline shapes. However, in its older mode, Hagal also corresponds to the Caduceus staff of Hermes/Mercury and the imagery of the world serpent. St Mercury shares the same festival date as St Catherine— November 25, and St Catherine and Hekate both have their own wheel symbolism; Hagal, too, has its own wheel symbolism. The mystic wheel of Hagal has, as its centrepiece, an ancient model of the mother rune in the form of a hexagramic cross constructed out of three intersecting oblong shapes— two diagonal and one vertical. This is surrounded by the more classical Hexagram in the form of a six-pointed star, as depicted in Hebrew symbolism. These are then encompassed by two circles containing eight symbols which denote the eight witches' sabbats or festivals in the year. In other words the mystic wheel of Hagal is another interpretation of the yearly cycle in the old pagan calendar.

Hagal is one of the most prominent runes of the Wyrd. The Wyrd relates to the cosmos, and a part of its solar symbolism involves not only three stars in Orion's belt but also the seven stars of the Pleiades known as the Boar's Throng—the boar being one of the most sacred animals in old northern folklore. In the northern tradition the stellar year began with Pleiades.

Once more, Mary's words concerning the Friends of Hekate and the old condition of the Old Worship, with its mystical stellar links, were proving to be correct.

The Ravaged Hill
The modern day Friends of Hekate/Dark Council were probably linked more to the methods and modus operandi of the wheel-based Templar organization than they were to witchcraft or Satanism, yet their roots had

definitely been laid in corrupt forms of the latter two.

The so-called magical power that they are trying to harness for their own purposes could best be described neither as ley power, orgone, subterranean, lunar or solar, but drawing from a combination of all these factors, coupled with the existing life force and static electricity contained within the human body and activated through ritual by the psycho-interaction of the human mind with all these elements.

While these modern-day practitioners of the Dark Worship continue to corrupt the old pagan festivals for their own purpose, what they are doing has nothing whatsoever to do with modern forms of paganism—indeed most modern pagans abhor the apparent desecration of ancient sites by such as the Dark Council/Friends of Hekate, and have tried to counteract these corrupt occultists accordingly, as we have seen at West Kennett; but in some cases they have been too late. St Catherine's Hill, Winchester, had been named as the 'hub' of the wheel in the Friends of Hekate's activities. During the course of Andrew Collins's surveillance of St Catherine's Hill in 1989, Helen had stated that the reformed Friends of Hekate 'were destroying it on an etheric level'.

However, the shocking reality is that in 1994 the government's massive road-building plans had achieved precisely that, though not exactly in the manner that she had described.

The now infamous extension of the M3 motorway at Twyford Down in effect disembowelled St Catherine's Hill, destroying it for all time. On a recent visit to this iniquitous man-made 'spaghetti junction', I pondered that very point. Helen's omens of destruction for this ancient site had physically and practically come to pass.

The process of accumulation and escalation of occult forces occurring over the next decade by such as the groups within the wheel, could well decide the fate of some of the other sites we had been looking at—but on an etheric level, as Helen had previously pointed out.

However, all the time I was reminded of Mary's words—that there was nothing like the power of positive thought and similar forms of meditation to defeat the negative energies raised by the Friends of Hekate. Positive powers used in this manner could, she was in fact saying, prevent the integrity and spiritual destiny of the country and the environment from falling into the hands of those who would darken and destroy it for their own ends.

Mary had first spoken of this need for 'positive power' back in 1984. A decade further on it seemed to us that now more than ever, and in the forthcoming years, was the time to use positive thought in order to win through.

Chapter 14
The Clandestine Global Controllers

The more I thought about the notion of using positive thought power to repel the wheel, with its murky cross-linkage of occult orders, the more I wondered about its current intentions.

Given that Hekate, Hagal and the Dark Goddesses of the underworld all had their own wheel symbolism, were there any other forms of ancient knowledge that were being corrupted in this way? If so, was I any closer to discovering what was currently going on?

In his recently published works on international conspiracies, David Icke, now a leading figure in unearthing deep-rooted and intertwined secret groups, looks at organizations that could have some relevance to the wheel.

In 1891 Cecil Rhodes, who gave his name to Rhodesia (now Zimbabwe), founded an elite institution, known as the Round Table, which was to be at the heart of both business and banking. David Icke maintains that after Rhodes's death in 1902, his original inception was taken over by the Illuminati—a surreptitious association consisting of some corrupt occultists and others whom Icke believed were part of an interlinking world power, embodying other groups he named, such as the Black Nobility.

The master plan was to create a one-world order by methods of manipulation and deceit so that the prospective global supremacists would become just that while the rest of us remained under their control; but it is not quite as simple as that.

In order to try and achieve this, these people are engaged in operating various repressive systems on a large-scale basis. One such plan is to lend money through various banking cartels serving as outlets to both sides in military conflict. The losers will obviously need more funds for rebuilding their devastated homeland, while the cost of winning a war can be nearly as great. There can be only one winner in all of this—the Illuminati. They perpetually add to the debts of the masses, and in so doing create vast amounts of wealth for themselves.

The Dark Worship

In ... *And the Truth Shall Set You Free* David Icke provides a detailed exposure of these alleged conspiratorial organizations. For its part the Round Table is an order within several orders. One of its surrounding groups is named the Bilderberg Group. The Round Table is pivotal to the others, with an inner circle who are aware of the master plan and various outer circle members in the other adjoining groups, most of whom are the inner circles lackeys but without realizing it or knowing quite what the big picture entails.

Looking at the diagram reproduced in David Icke's books, showing the Round Table surrounded and protected by its 'front groups', I was immediately reminded of the Hekate Wheel drawing—symbolically, at any rate.

Back in 1990 Andrew Collins had been warned by one of his associates that the Wheel had been the power behind some of the most atrocious acts of mankind, and that they were much more than an organization in the accepted sense. Now David Icke was saying much the same about the Round Table/Illuminati/Black Nobility interconnections.

The obvious question was: were they all one and the same thing? Answer: quite possibly, but it was still impossible to say. One thing, however, was for certain. Both sets of groups used exactly the same methods of organization and infrastructure—notably the malefic power spiral.

That is the system of circles and grades that allows the inner sanctum to remain protected while outer-circle members carry on oblivious to what the central hierarchy is really up to.

According to David Icke, the elite who operate at the top of the Illuminati network, are interacting with dark forces. He states that many of them belong to extreme sects based on ancient rites and Lucifer/Satan worship. He goes on to say that 'If you infiltrated some of these bizarre gatherings, I am sure you would see some very famous faces'.

And David Icke wasn't the only author with such a perilous quest in mind. Award-winning writer and documentary film-maker Jon Ronson decided to look further into such claims, which were being echoed by many at opposite ends of the political spectrum, particularly in the USA. The results were screened on Britain's Channel 4 and published in a book by Jon Ronson entitled *Them: Adventures with Extremists* (2001).

The Owl and the Pussycats

Bohemian Grove is a 2700-acre site whose location is not printed on conventional maps of the area. It forms part of a clearing in a forest of huge redwood trees seventy-five miles north of San Francisco in California. Access is restricted to a lane accompanied by a sign that reads 'No Through

Road'. Private security personnel are also in attendance to ensure that no one does go through, but why all the secrecy?

This is the place where, according to speculation, the rulers of the world meet up, don hooded robes and partake in secret pagan or corrupt occult rituals. People in the Bilderberg group are directly involved, according to some sources; the Round Table, too. I recall a telephone conversation that I'd had with David Icke some time ago concerning my first book, *The Demonic Connection*. We had soon got on to the subject of 'international network Satanism', for want of a better phrase, and he was quite adamant that this went 'straight to the top in the States'.

It was therefore not surprising that the names of American presidents, including the Bush dynasty, were all linked to the goings-on at Bohemian Grove—whatever that might be; very few, if any, people who weren't directly involved had ever witnessed these goings on and come back to tell the tale. Jon Ronson and his assembled associates would soon discover the truth.

Posing as participants by wearing carefully chosen casual clothing, Jon Ronson and his colleagues had managed to trick the security guard into letting them through. This had been largely engineered by one of the group, American radio and TV talk-show host Alex Jones, who had smuggled concealed video cameras into the Grove by taking a different route through the forest, avoiding security guards and hidden security cameras placed in the trees.

They witnessed a ritual known as the 'Cremation of Care', performed by a gold and silver robed high priest and relayed through loudspeakers secreted in the nearby trees. At the sound of drums exploding from the speakers, approximately thirty black-robed figures carrying burning torches emerged from the trees, each figure appearing to the accompaniment of a roaring drumbeat. The supposed inner-circle initiates then lit a fire at the foot of a massive fifty-foot stone horned owl—the so-called shrine. There had been much talk of an owl-burning ceremony and sacrifice from various sources during Jon Ronson's preliminary enquiries; he would soon know the accuracy of what he had been told.

Sure enough, amid bizarre theatrics, a Death figure could be seen floating in a gondola on the nearby lagoon and carrying a paper dummy, which was virtually life-size. The high priest had made references to 'Dull Care' being slain immediately for the benefit of those present. This was a yearly event and had echoes of John Barleycorn, but the method here was much more in tune with the Lammas fire ritual. The large paper effigy representing Dull Care was then offered to the owl before being discarded into the fire amid loud cheers from the ensemble. Jon Ronson and his colleagues had doubted whether there was anything—or anyone, for that matter—inside the paper effigy. The symbolic sacrifice, though, had seemed real enough, and in this situation one could never be sure of anything. Police investigations into purported murders at Bohemian Grove had come to nothing.

Back in their hotel rooms Jon Ronson and Alex Jones debated what they had witnessed, including the question of symbolic human sacrifice, with differing conclusions. Jon Ronson took the ceremony to indicate a ritual burning of the burdens and business responsibilities of the 'Grovers'. There were about a thousand or so present at the ritual, who were mostly invited onlookers. He had seen some older-looking men dressed in rather grotesque drag outfits, while elsewhere, prior to the main ritual, he had observed others leaping about to a live band playing 1950s rock'n'roll classics. No harm in that. Were these elderly looking gents merely a bunch of old pussycats just letting their hair down? Not so, according to Alex Jones. He claims that they were 'burning a human in effigy'—a simulated sacrifice to their great owl god.

The sacrificial victim, Dull Care, can be heard over the speaker system pleading for his life in a death-rattle voice. Looking at the video footage shown in the TV programme, I had been aware of the menacing tones in the voices of the leading figures as they enacted the ritual. Jon Ronson had also noted that despite its natural beauty, Bohemian Grove's 'ambience' seemed deliberately spooky—almost calculatingly created to portray a druidic/satanic atmosphere. So were there any further clues as to what lay behind all this?

The 'Cremation of Care' ritual was supposed to be a midsummer's event; it actually took place on July 15, 2000, marking the festival of Rowana, the patroness of the arcane runic knowledge who is also the tree goddess. Part of the Bohemian Grove ritual involved references to trees and natural wood. Sanctified fires for important rituals were linked to the use of rowan, oak or yew wood—particularly for druidic rites. Rowan imagery had previously been found at the West Kennett Long Barrow (see Chapter 12), where, among others, a line of runic glyphs spelling 'ROWAN' was deliberately chalked next to an inverted pentagram on the wall of the west chamber; its exact purpose remains a mystery.

Owls are regarded as mysterious birds owing to their predatory, nocturnal ways, so it is not surprising that they accorded it a place in occult symbolism. Besides the fifty-foot stone owl at the Bohemian Grove altar, there are other smaller wooden ones placed at various points in the same locality.

The 18th-century artist and poet William Blake portrayed Hekate as

Queen of the Witches, and showed her being accompanied by her messengers—among others, an owl. Owls were also considered to be the witches' familiar or incarnation. In Welsh mythology the owl is called *adern y corff* or corpse-bird, while in Scottish Gaelic it is known as *cailleach oidhche*, which translates as 'night-hag'. Cailleach is, of course, the death goddess and is linked to both Hekate and Kali (see Chapter 12). The owl also featured in some of the early Celtic and European cults, though mainly as a goddess type. The gold terminals of a torque (ancient metal collar or neck chain) dating to *c.* 400 BC, and discovered in the grave of a princess at Reinheim near Saarbrucken, Germany, depict a goddess with an owl emerging from her head.

The owl is also the symbol of Moloch, whom the Greeks compared to Cronos on account of Moloch's rites using human sacrifices, especially children and first-born infants. The Old Testament makes references to the Valley of Hinnom as the area where fires were lit beneath the idol or image of Moloch, into which the unfortunate sacrificial victims were thrown. The precise location of these sacrifices is known as Topheth, which originates from the Hebrew *toph*, meaning 'drum'—drums were ostensibly used to cover up the screams of the victims.

In the cabbalistic custom, Moloch and Satan were at the top of the ten evil Sephiroth, representing the negative facet of Kether, the first Sephiroth, also called the 'crown of knowledge'.

Drums, of course, figured quite prominently in part of the Bohemian Grove ritual, as did the lighting of a sacrificial pyre beneath a stone idol.

Perhaps the most potent symbolism can be found in the Egyptian hieroglyphic method, where owls represent death and blackness. They relate to the 'dead sun', which has set beneath the horizon that crosses the lake or sea of darkness.

The owl ritual at Bohemian Grove took place at dusk and involved the use of practically the same type of imagery as the Egyptian system.

This is a firm indication that despite the obvious theatrics, there was more significance to the owl ritual than some may have at first thought.

In a sense, both Jon Ronson and Alex Jones are correct in their interpretations of the ritual at Bohemian Grove. Looking at the video footage, the ceremony's main theme had its roots resolutely placed in the old pagan tradition of kingship or substitute symbolic sacrifice by fire, in accordance with ancient fertility rites, as part of the yearly wheel-turning cycle. In this case, however, the words 'ancient fertility' can be replaced by 'modern business cares and responsibilities'.

The list of 'Bohemian Grovers' reads like a recently documented White

The Dark Worship

House history, with photographs showing Richard Nixon and Ronald Reagan in attendance at the Grove, and the names of many other leading political figures from both sides of the Atlantic, including current US Vice-President Dick Cheney and President George W. Bush himself.

Why are the leaders and hierarchical patrons of vast Christian-based democracies embracing something that has its origins firmly entrenched in a dark ritual past?

Are the conspiracy theorists right?

If so, the wheel is turning...

Illustration Credits

Photographs

1–6   Author's photographs.

7   The goat's jawbone was found by Charles Walker and photographed by the author.

8, 9   Charles Walker.

10   Andrew Collins.

11   Scottish rite: 18th-degree masonic ritual taken from *A Pictorial History of Magic and the Supernatural*, ed. Maurice Bessy (Spring Books/Hamlyn, 1964).

12, 13   *The Ritual Killing of Thomas Becket* and *Absolution for the Incarnate God* are both taken from *The Roots of Witchcraft* by Michael Harrison (Frederick Muller, 1973).

Line Drawings

1   The Hekate Wheel, from *Magical and Mystical Sites in Europe and the British Isles* by Elizabeth Pepper and John Wilcock (BCA, 1977).

2   *The Ancient British Wheel* by Richard Elen courtesy of Kathy Jones from her book *The Ancient British Goddess* (Ariadne Publications, 1991).

3   St Catherine's Wheel from *Saints, Signs and Symbols* by W. Ellwood Post (SPCK, 1966).

4   The voodoo 'Damballah' from *A Pictorial History of Magic and the Supernatural*, ed. Maurice Bessy (Spring Books/Hamlyn, 1964).

5   The runic message and inverted pentagram were originally chalked in white, taken from video footage shot by Charles Walker and redrawn in black by the author.

Bibliography

AA Illustrated Guide to Britain (Drive Publications, 1971)

Ahmed, Rollo, *The Black Art* (John Long, 1936)

Ashe, Geoffrey, *The Ancient Wisdom* (Macmillan, 1977)

Baigent, Michael and Leigh, Richard, *The Temple and the Lodge* (Jonathan Cape, 1989)

Barber, Richard, *Henry Plantagenet* (Boydell Press, 1964)

Barber, Richard, *The Devil's Crown* (BBC Books, 1978)

Begg, Ean, *The Cult of the Black Virgin* (Arcane, 1985)

Bentley, James, *Secrets of Mount Sinai* (Orbis, 1985)

Bessy, Maurice, ed., *A Pictorial History of Magic and the Supernatural* (Hamlyn, 1964)

Bord, Janet, and Colin, *Mysterious Britain* (Paladin, 1974)

Bord, Janet and Colin, *The Secret Country* (Paladin, 1978)

Brookesmith, Peter, ed., *Cult and Occult* (Orbis, 1980)

Cavendish, Richard, *The Black Arts* (Pan, 1969)

Cavendish, Richard, *A History of Magic* (Sphere, 1978)

Cirlot, J. E., *A Dictionary of Symbols* (Routledge and Kegan Paul, 1962)

Collins, Andrew, *The Black Alchemist* (ABC Books, 1988)

Collins, Andrew, *The Seventh Sword* (Century, 1991)

Collins, Andrew, *The Second Coming* (Arrow, 1993)

Conway, David, *The Secret Wisdom* (Jonathan Cape, 1985)

Cotterell, Arthur, *The Illustrated Encyclopedia of Myths and Legends* (Guild Publishing, 1985)

Crow, W. B., *A History of Magic Witchcraft and Occultism* (Aquarian Press, 1968)

Davidson, Revd I. E., *Readings in Revelation* (Barbican Book Room, 1969)

Encyclopedia of Witchcraft and Demonology (Octopus Books, 1974)

Farrar, Janet and Stewart, *Eight Sabbats for Witches* (Washington DC, 1981)

Farrar, Janet and Stewart, *The Witches' Way* (Guild, 1985)

Farrar, Janet and Stewart, *The Witches' Goddess* (Robert Hale, 1987)

Gettings, Fred, *Encyclopedia of the Occult* (BCA, 1986)

Gettings, Fred, *Dictionary of Demons* (Guild, 1988)

Gooch, Stan, *Guardians of the Ancient Wisdom* (Wildwood House, 1979)

Goodricke-Clarke, Nicholas, *The Occult Roots of Nazism* (Aquarian Press, 1985)

Grant, Kenneth, *Cults of the Shadow* (Frederick Muller, 1975)

Graves, Robert, *The Greek Myths* (Penguin Books, 1948)

Green, J. R., *A Short History of the English People* (Macmillan, 1889)

Greene, Liz, *The Astrology of Fate* (George Allen & Unwin, 1984)

Grillot de Givry, Emile, *Illustrated Anthology of Sorcery, Magic and Alchemy* (Zachary Kwinter, 1991)

Grinnel-Milne, Duncan, *The Killing of William Rufus* (David and Charles, 1979)

Guerber, H. A., *The Norsemen* (Gresham Publishing, 1994)

Haining, Peter, *Witchcraft and Black Magic* (Paul Hamlyn, 1971)

Hall, Frederic T., *The Pedigree of the Devil* (Trubner & Co, 1883)

Hallam, Elizabeth, ed., *The Plantagenet Chronicles* (Tiger Books, 1995)

Harrison, Michael, *The Roots of Witchcraft* (Frederick Muller, 1973)

Howard, Michael, *The Wisdom of the Runes* (Rider, 1985)

Howard, Michael, *The Occult Conspiracy* (Rider, 1989)

Hyatt, Victoria and Charles, Joseph W., *The Book of Demons* (Lorrimer, 1974)

Icke, David, *The Biggest Secret* (Bridge of Love, 1991)

Icke, David, *Love Changes Everything* (Aquarian Press, 1992)

Icke, David, *Robots' Rebellion* (Gateway Books, 1994)

Icke, David, *...And the Truth Shall Set You Free* (Bridge of Love, 1995)

James, Geoffrey, *The Enochian Magick of Dr John Dee* (Llewellyn Publications, MN, 1994)

Jenkins, Stephen, *The Undiscovered Country* (Collins, 1976)

Jones, Kathy, *The Ancient British Goddess* (Ariadne Publications, 1991)

Kenyon, Theda, *Witches Still Live* (Rider, 1931)

Knight, Gareth, *A History of White Magic* (A. R. Mowbray and Co., 1978)

Line, Julia, *Discover Numerology* (Aquarian Press, 1992)

Mackenzie, Norman, ed., *Secret Societies* (Aldus, n. d.)

Maclellan, Alex, *The Lost World of Agharti* (Souvenir, 1982)

Maple, Eric, *The Dark World of Witches* (Robert Hale, 1962)

Maple, Eric, *The Domain of Devils* (Robert Hale, 1966)

Maple, Eric, *Supernatural England* (Robert Hale, 1977)

Marshall, Richard, *The History and Mythology of Witchcraft* (Magna, 1995)

Michaud, J. *The Golden Star* (UMA Press, 1946)

Bibliography

Murray, Dr Margaret, *The God of the Witches* (Daimon Press, 1962)

New Larousse Encyclopedia of Mythology (Paul Hamlyn, 1959)

O'Grady, Joan, *The Prince of Darkness* (Element, 1989)

Parker, John, *At The Heart of Darkness* (Sidgwick & Jackson, 1993)

Pennick, Nigel, *The Pagan Source Book* (Rider, 1992)

Pennick, Nigel, *Runic Astrology* (Capall Bann, 1995)

Pepper, Elizabeth, Wilcock, John, *Magical and Mystical Sites in Europe and the British Isles* (BCA, 1977)

Poole, Austin Lane, *From Domesday Book to Magna Carta, 1087–1216* (Clarendon Press, 1955)

Ravenscroft, Trevor, *The Spear of Destiny* (Neville Spearman, 1973)

Roderick, Timothy, *Dark Moon Mysteries* (Llewellyn Publications, MN, 1996)

Ronan, Stephen, *The Goddess Hekate* (Chthonios Books, 1992)

Ronson, Jon, *Them: Adventures with Extremists* (Picador, 2001)

Ross, Anne, *Pagan Celtic Britain* (Sphere, 1974)

Russell, Jeffrey B, *A History of Witchcraft, Sorcerers, Heretics and Pagans* (Thames and Hudson, 1980)

Satan (Sheed and Ward, 1951)

Seligman, Kurt, *Magic, Supernaturalism and Religion* (Allen Lane, 1971)

Short, Martin, *Inside the Brotherhood* (Grafton, 1989)

Spence, Lewis, *An Introduction to Mythology* (George G. Harrap, 1921)

Spence, Lewis, *The Mysteries of Britain* (Rider, 1925)

Spence, Lewis, *The Encyclopedia of the Occult* (Bracken Books, 1994)

Summers, Montague, *Geography of Witchcraft* (University Books, New York, 1958)

Temple, Robert, *The Sirius Mystery* (Destiny Books, Vermont, 1998)

Thompson, Rev. J. L., *That Glorious Future* (Morgan and Scott, *c.* 1890)

Thorsson, Edred, *Futhark* (Samuel Weiser Inc., York Beach, 1994)

Tomas, Andrew, *Shambhalla, Oasis of Light* (Sphere, 1977)

Tondriau, J. and Villeneuve, R. *A Dictionary of Devils and Demons* (Tom Stacey, 1972)

Valiente, Doreen, *An ABC of Witchcraft Past and Present* (Robert Hale, 1973)

Waite, A. E., *The Book of Black Magic* (Samuel Weiser Inc., York Beach, 1989)

Wallace-Murphy, Tim and Ravenscroft, Trevor, *The Mark of the Beast* (Sphere, 1990)

Wheatley, Dennis, *The Devil and All His Works* (Hutchinson, 1971)

Whitlock, Ralph, *In Search of Lost Gods* (Phaidon Press, 1979)

Wilcock, John, *A Guide to Occult Britain* (Sidgwick and Jackson, 1976)

Willis, Tony, *Discover Runes* (Aquarian Press, 1991)

Woods, William, *A History of the Devil* (W. H. Allen, 1973)

Index

Index

Index